THE TRANSFORMATION MINDSET

REWIRE BELIEFS.
EMBED BEHAVIORS.
LEAD THE MOVEMENT.

MANISH PHARASI

ISBN
Paperback 979-8-89777-885-0
Hardcase 979-8-89929-698-7

Contents

Preface

Transformation is more than a buzzword. It's a journey—sometimes messy, often unpredictable, and always personal. Over the course of my career, I've had the privilege of walking alongside leaders confronting disruption, organizations navigating uncertainty, and teams striving to unlock their true potential. Through these experiences, one truth has consistently surfaced: **transformation isn't driven by tools, frameworks, or even talent alone—it's driven by mindset.**

The seeds of this book were planted in boardroom debates, workshop breakthroughs, and vulnerable one-on-one conversations. I've witnessed the fear of failure, the weight of legacy thinking, and the paralysis that often comes with complexity. But I've also seen something far more powerful: the courage to reimagine, the willingness to learn, and the resilience to lead forward. It was in these moments that I felt compelled to go deeper—to explore the science, psychology, and practical mechanics of what makes transformation truly stick.

This book is the result of that pursuit. It blends behavioral science, neuroscience, and hard-earned lessons from real-world practice. It's written for leaders, change agents, and anyone who's ever wondered why transformation feels so difficult—and how it can finally be made sustainable.

Why This Book, and Why Now

Every leader I have worked with has had the same aspiration: to create lasting impact. And yet, many are held back by invisible forces—entrenched beliefs, cultural inertia, and the very systems they helped build. These aren't isolated challenges. They're systemic, cross-industry, and deeply human. That's what makes them solvable—with the right lens.

This book was born out of a desire to bridge the **knowing–doing gap**. To move beyond inspiration and into implementation. What emerged is the **Catalyst Framework**—a five-phase approach that doesn't just guide change but reconditions mindsets to make change sustainable. It's not a rigid formula. It's a mindset-first methodology that's adaptable, inclusive, and designed to work in the real world.

What You'll Find in These Pages

The book is divided into two parts:

- **Part 1: Foundations of Transformation** explores the neuroscience and psychology behind why we resist change—and how to rewire those patterns.

- **Part 2: The Catalyst Framework** offers a practical, five-phase roadmap: **Analyze, Reframe, Design, Execute, and Sustain**—each rooted in both theory and tested application.

Throughout the book, you'll find real-world examples, stories from global organizations, and practical prompts to turn insight into action. This is not a book to read passively. It's a toolkit for reflective, courageous, and systemic transformation.

With Gratitude

This book is shaped by the leaders who've trusted me during some of their most challenging moments. Your stories, struggles, and successes are what make these pages breathe.

To the behavioral scientists and neuroscientists whose work has profoundly influenced this framework—thank you. Your insights have lit the path to a more human, sustainable approach to change.

And to my family, friends, and colleagues—thank you for your unwavering support. Your belief in this mission has been my anchor and my fuel.

A Personal Call to Action

This book is more than a guide—it's an invitation.

An invitation to rewire how you think about change.

To challenge what's always been done.

To transform not just your organization, but your leadership, your culture, and yourself.

The Transformation Mindset: Rewire Beliefs. Embed Behaviors. Lead the Movement is built on a simple but powerful idea: sustainable transformation doesn't start with systems—it starts with mindsets. If we want different results, we must think differently, act intentionally, and lead with courage.

Whether you're a CEO guiding enterprise-wide change, a team leader rebuilding culture, or a professional rethinking your own growth—you are a catalyst.

This book is your roadmap.

Let's begin.

Introduction: Why Transformation Begins with the Mind

In an increasingly unpredictable and rapidly evolving world, the ability to adapt and transform is no longer a luxury—it is a necessity. For organizations, leaders, and individuals alike, transformation is not merely about reacting to external changes but about anticipating them, thriving amid uncertainty, and seizing opportunities for growth. Yet, for many, the idea of transformation is daunting, cloaked in resistance, fear, and doubt.

Consider this: A Fortune 500 company on the brink of obsolescence faced plummeting revenues and a workforce resistant to change. Its leadership turned to an innovative approach—one rooted not in technology or strategy but in transforming mindsets. By reshaping limiting beliefs, fostering adaptability, and realigning behaviors, the organization was able to not only survive but emerge stronger, igniting a culture of innovation and collaboration. What changed wasn't just the business—it was how people thought, acted, and led. This is the power of the **transformation mindset**.

This book is about cultivating that mindset—a powerful, science-backed approach to unlocking potential and driving meaningful, lasting change. It's about moving beyond superficial fixes and embracing transformation as a mindset, a practice, and a way of life.

The Foundation of Transformation: Why Mindset Matters

At its core, transformation begins in the mind. The way we think influences the way we act, and the way we act shapes our outcomes.

Modern neuroscience offers us profound insights into this connection. Our brains, once thought to be static and unchangeable, are now known to possess remarkable plasticity. **Neuroplasticity**, the brain's ability to rewire itself in response to experiences and behaviors, underscores the incredible capacity we have to adapt, grow, and transform.

However, neuroplasticity is a double-edged sword. The same mechanisms that allow us to create new pathways can also reinforce unproductive habits, behaviors, and mindsets if left unchecked. In the workplace, this manifests as entrenched silos, resistance to change, and limiting beliefs such as "this is how we've always done it." These patterns are not merely organizational—they are neurological.

The good news? Just as these pathways are formed, they can be rewired. Through deliberate effort, repetition, and reinforcement, individuals and organizations can break free from the inertia of "wrong wiring" and create new pathways that foster growth, adaptability, and resilience. This book explores the intersection of neuroscience and transformation, showing you how to leverage the principles of neuroplasticity to rewire not only your brain but also your teams and organizations.

From Foundations to Action: What This Book Offers

Transformation is as much about mindset as it is about action. This book is divided into two parts, each designed to guide you through the journey of unlocking potential and driving change:

Part 1: The Foundations of Transformation

We begin by exploring the inner workings of transformation—how the brain rewires itself, how beliefs and behaviors form, and how these patterns shape the workplace.

In this section, you'll discover:

- How **neuroplasticity** enables change and why it's essential for both personal and organizational transformation.

- How **limiting beliefs**—such as "change is too hard" or "failure is not an option"—subtly block progress.

- How to **challenge these beliefs** and replace them with empowering narratives that drive action.

- The four defining traits of a transformation mindset—**adaptability, curiosity, resilience, and empowerment**—and how leaders can cultivate them in themselves and others.

Grounded in science and real-world examples, Part 1 helps you understand why transformation begins in the mind—and how to prepare the ground before planting the seeds of change.

Part 2: The Catalyst for Action

Once the foundation is set, we move into action.

Part 2 introduces the **Catalyst Framework**—a practical, five-phase roadmap for translating mindset shifts into measurable outcomes. Whether you're driving change within a team or across an entire organization, this framework gives you a repeatable process to guide the journey.

You'll learn how to:

1. **Analyze**: Surface the invisible barriers and hidden narratives that block change.

2. **Reframe**: Shift anti-stories—internalized beliefs that limit action—into powerful new narratives.

3. **Design**: Build systems and behaviors rooted in behavioral science to reinforce the new mindset.

4. **Execute**: Translate plans into disciplined action, anchored in ownership and feedback loops.

5. **Sustain**: Reinforce, adapt, and scale success so transformation becomes part of your culture.

Packed with practical tools, field-tested strategies, and case studies from global organizations, Part 2 turns insight into action—and action into sustained impact.

Why This Book Matters Now

The world of work has changed. Leaders are navigating challenges that are more complex and dynamic than ever before—global disruptions, technological advancements, evolving employee expectations, and shifting societal norms. In this environment, traditional approaches to transformation often fall short because they focus on surface-level fixes rather than addressing the root cause: the way people think and behave.

The **transformation mindset** is the antidote. It enables leaders to embrace change not as a disruption but as an opportunity. It empowers teams to collaborate, innovate, and execute with clarity and confidence. It creates a culture where transformation becomes second nature, unlocking the potential of both individuals and organizations.

By combining the latest insights from neuroscience, behavioral science, and leadership practice, this book offers a fresh perspective on transformation. It challenges you to rethink how you approach change, providing you with the knowledge and tools to inspire action, overcome resistance, and achieve sustainable results.

An Invitation to Transform

This book is not just a guide—it's a call to action. Whether you are a CEO leading a large-scale organizational change, a manager striving to build a high-performing team, or an individual seeking personal growth, the principles in this book are for you.

Imagine what could be achieved if you and your organization embraced transformation as a mindset—a lens through which challenges become opportunities, setbacks become learning moments, and change becomes a catalyst for growth. Imagine leading with clarity, fostering collaboration, and achieving results that not only meet but exceed expectations.

The journey to transformation starts here, with the decision to think differently, act decisively, and lead authentically. As you turn the pages of this book, you'll gain not just insights but practical tools to make transformation a reality in your work and life.

Let's embark on this journey together. Let's unlock potential. Let's drive change.

Welcome to the Transformation Mindset.

Part I:

The Inner Shift — Building the Transformation Mindset

Chapter 1:

Understanding Neuroplasticity

Imagine standing at the edge of a dense forest. Before you lies a single, well-worn path winding through the trees. It's familiar and easy to follow, but what if this path doesn't lead to your destination? You could stick to it, retracing the same steps over and over, or you could carve a new trail—one that is harder at first but offers a faster, more direct route to where you need to go.

This image of the forest is a powerful metaphor for how the brain works. For years, scientists believed that the brain was like that well-worn path—fixed and unchanging, locked into the patterns formed early in life. But modern neuroscience has revolutionized our understanding of the brain, revealing it to be dynamic, adaptable, and capable of incredible change at any age. This ability to "carve new trails" is called neuroplasticity, and it holds the key to personal and organizational transformation.

Neuroplasticity teaches us a profound truth: change is possible. Whether it's an individual trying to break free from self-doubt or an organization seeking to shift deeply ingrained cultural patterns, the principles of neuroplasticity show us that transformation isn't just a hopeful idea—it's a scientific reality. But, like carving a new trail through a forest, it takes effort, intention, and repetition.

Throughout this chapter, we'll explore what neuroplasticity is, how it works, and why it's so central to the journey of transformation. From rewiring individual habits to reshaping workplace cultures, neuroplasticity provides a roadmap for creating new pathways—both in the mind and in the systems, we build around us.

What Readers Will Learn

In this chapter, you'll discover:

- How neuroplasticity enables the brain to rewire itself in response to thoughts, actions, and experiences.

- The three key principles of neuroplasticity—repetition, reinforcement, and exposure—and their role in driving change.

- Real-life stories of individuals and organizations applying neuroplasticity to overcome challenges and achieve growth.

- Actionable insights to help you start applying these principles in your personal and professional life.

By the end of this chapter, you'll understand not only how change is possible but also how to take the first steps toward it. Whether you're navigating a personal challenge or leading a team through organizational transformation, neuroplasticity offers the tools to carve a new trail and chart a course toward success.

The Science Behind Neuroplasticity

At its core, **neuroplasticity** is the brain's extraordinary ability to adapt by forming and reorganizing neural connections. Far from being hardwired at birth, the human brain is more like a dynamic system—constantly shaped by what we think, feel, say, and do. Neuroplasticity is the biological foundation for growth, learning, and change. It is also what makes transformation—not only possible, but sustainable.

What Are Neurons and How Do They Communicate?

Our brains are made up of billions of neurons—specialized cells that transmit information through electrical and chemical signals. When we engage in a thought, emotion, or action, a specific group of neurons "fire" together, sending messages across tiny gaps called synapses.

Over time, if those neurons keep firing together in a consistent pattern, they begin to wire together—forming stronger, faster connections. This process is governed by a foundational principle of neuroscience known as **Hebb's Rule**, often summed up as:

"Neurons that fire together, wire together."

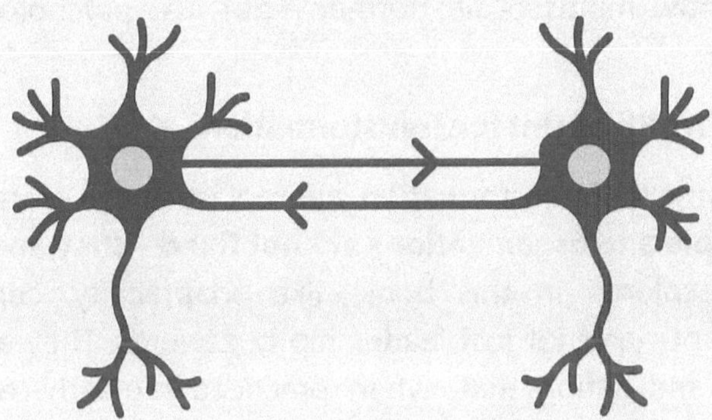

How Neural Pathways Are Formed – and Hardwired

Imagine your brain as a dense network of roads. Every thought, reaction, or behavior is like a car traveling along those roads. The more often you take a particular route—say, reacting defensively in meetings or hesitating to speak up—the smoother and faster that road becomes. Eventually, it becomes your default highway, even if it's not taking you where you want to go.

The same applies to empowering behaviors. If you consistently practice curiosity, adapt to change, or show resilience under pressure, those pathways strengthen too. Repetition builds efficiency, turning conscious effort into subconscious habit.

Here's the key insight:

Whatever we repeatedly think, feel, or do becomes physically embedded in our brain's wiring.

This is how mindsets are formed—not just psychologically, but biologically.

The Brain's Blueprint for Transformation

In the context of transformation, neuroplasticity gives us a powerful insight: **people and organizations are not fixed—they are rewirable.** The traits explored in this book—like adaptability, curiosity, and empowerment—are not just leadership buzzwords. They are patterns of thought and action that, when practiced regularly, reshape our internal wiring.

That means the change we seek isn't about forcing people to adopt new tools or processes. It's about helping them form new neural pathways—**from resistance to resilience, from passivity to empowerment, from fear to forward motion.**

It's not just behavior change—it's brain change.

And it begins with one intentional thought, one conversation, one act of courage—**repeated.**

Example: The Power of Habit Formation

- **Positive Pathway:** An employee who receives positive reinforcement for collaboration strengthens the neural pathways associated with teamwork, making collaboration their default behavior.

- **Negative Pathway:** Conversely, a team working in a blame-filled culture develops pathways of avoidance and mistrust, reinforcing siloed thinking.

The good news is that these pathways are not permanent. With intentional effort, you can forge new trails that better align with your goals. This process of replacing old pathways with new ones lies at the heart of transformation.

Two Levels of Neuroplasticity

Neuroplasticity helps the brain adapt in **two ways**—one that provides a **quick boost** and another that creates **lasting change**.

Short-Term Adaptation (Quick Wins, But Temporary)

- When you learn something new, your brain fires up connections like a spark—quick but fleeting.

- This is why new ideas or habits feel exciting at first but fade if not reinforced.

- Example: A leader attends a workshop on active listening and feels motivated to apply it. But without continued practice, old habits resurface.

Long-Term Adaptation (Lasting Change)

- With repetition, the brain physically rewires itself, making a new habit automatic—like a well-trodden path.

- The more a behavior is practiced, the stronger and more effortless it becomes.

- Example: A team that consistently practices collaborative problem-solving hardwires it into their culture, making teamwork second nature.

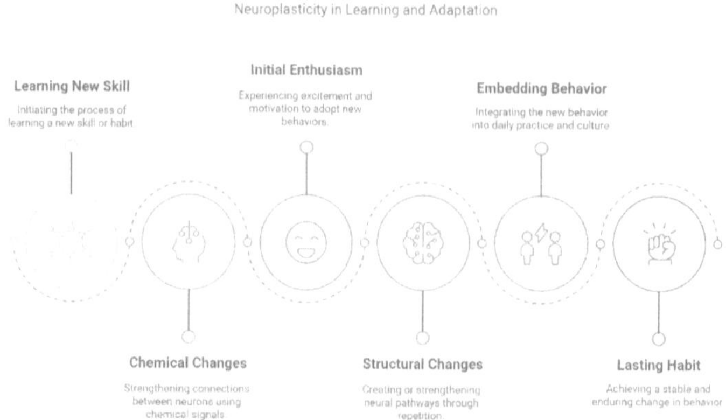

Key Insight:

Long-term transformation—whether for individuals or organizations—requires a commitment to repetition. The more you practice a new behavior, the stronger its neural pathway becomes.

The Role of Repetition, Reinforcement, and Exposure

Neuroplasticity is driven by three core principles, each of which plays a vital role in creating lasting change:

Three Core Principles of Neuroplasticity

Repetition
Strengthens
Pathways

Reinforcement
Shapes
Behavior

Exposure
Expands
Perspectives

1. **Repetition Strengthens Pathways:**

   - Just as walking the same trail in a forest makes it more defined, repeating a behavior strengthens its neural pathway. This is why small, consistent actions are more effective than sporadic, grand gestures.

   - *Example:* An individual practicing mindfulness for five minutes daily strengthens the neural pathways associated with focus and calm over time.

2. **Reinforcement Shapes Behavior:**

   - Behaviors that are rewarded—intentionally or unintentionally—are more likely to be repeated. Positive reinforcement strengthens neural connections, making desired behaviors more automatic.

   - *Example:* A manager who acknowledges team members for proactive problem-solving encourages repetition of that behavior, embedding it into the team's culture.

3. **Exposure Expands Possibilities:**

   - Exposure to new perspectives, environments, challenges, or collaborators activates unfamiliar neural circuits, allowing individuals and teams to rewire limiting patterns. Without exposure, old beliefs and routines dominate by default.

   - *Example:* A company transitioning to agile practices rotates team members across departments to expose them to different problem-solving approaches, accelerating collaboration and innovation.

These principles apply not just at the individual level—but also at scale. Just as one person can rewire a habit, entire teams and organizations can rewire how they think, decide, and behave.

Why Understanding Neuroplasticity Matters for Transformation

Understanding the science of neuroplasticity provides a roadmap for navigating change:

- **For Individuals:** It explains why breaking old habits feels difficult and how consistent effort can lead to breakthroughs.

- **For Organizations:** It reveals why deeply ingrained cultural patterns persist and how they can be reshaped through deliberate, systemic efforts.

As you continue this book, you'll see these principles applied to personal and organizational transformation, offering tools to help you forge new pathways in your own life and work.

Personal Transformation: Stories of Change

The principles of neuroplasticity are not just theoretical; they have real, profound impacts on individual lives. Whether overcoming fears, breaking old habits, or building new skills, personal transformation begins with the decision to carve new neural pathways and the persistence to reinforce them over time.

Let's explore the journeys of two individuals—Sarah and Priya— whose transformations illustrate the power of neuroplasticity in action.

Sarah's Journey: From Fear to Confidence

Sarah, a mid-level manager, had always dreaded public speaking. Her fear stemmed from an early experience when a presentation didn't go as planned, leaving her embarrassed in front of her peers. Over time, Sarah developed a neural pathway that associated public speaking with failure and anxiety. This pathway became a "superhighway" in her brain, making avoidance her automatic response whenever she was asked to present.

Determined to overcome this fear, Sarah embarked on a journey of deliberate rewiring:

1. **Repetition:** She practiced speaking in front of a mirror daily, starting with just a few sentences. Over time, she progressed to presenting in front of close friends and, eventually, small groups at work.

2. **Reinforcement:** Sarah sought constructive feedback after each attempt and celebrated small victories, such as completing a presentation without freezing.

3. **Exposure:** She joined a supportive public speaking group, where encouragement and camaraderie provided the safe space she needed to experiment and grow.

Within months, Sarah noticed a shift. The pathway of fear that once dominated her brain was gradually overridden by a new pathway of confidence. By the end of the year, Sarah was not only presenting in meetings but also volunteering to lead workshops—a testament to the power of intentional effort.

Priya's Transformation: Breaking Free from Impostor Syndrome

Priya, a senior leader in a tech firm, struggled with impostor syndrome despite her accomplishments. She often downplayed her achievements, convinced that her success was due to luck rather than ability. This belief created a self-reinforcing loop: Priya avoided high-visibility projects, which limited her opportunities for recognition, further cementing her feelings of inadequacy.

Priya decided to take control of her narrative by rewiring her mindset:

1. **Repetition:** Every morning, she practiced self-affirmations, reminding herself of her strengths and contributions.

2. **Reinforcement:** Priya began sharing her successes with trusted colleagues, whose positive feedback helped shift her perspective.

3. **Reflection:** She kept a journal where she documented moments of growth and courage, such as stepping out of her comfort zone to lead a challenging project.

Over time, these deliberate practices rewired Priya's neural pathways. She began to see herself not as an impostor but as a capable and deserving leader. Within a year, Priya was confidently taking on high-profile projects and inspiring her peers with her leadership.

Lessons from Sarah and Priya

Sarah and Priya's stories highlight three critical principles of neuroplasticity:

1. **Start Small:** Both women began with manageable steps—short speeches for Sarah and daily affirmations for Priya—that gradually built momentum.

2. **Reinforce Positivity:** Constructive feedback and self-reflection helped them strengthen their new neural pathways.

3. **Seek Diverse Exposure:** Both women accelerated their growth by stepping outside their comfort zones—Sarah joined a public speaking group, and Priya engaged with colleagues who challenged her thinking. Exposure to new perspectives and experiences helped rewire their beliefs and broaden their confidence.

Reflection for Readers

- What personal habits or beliefs have you developed over time?

- Are there any that no longer serve you, and how might you begin to rewire them?

These stories demonstrate that the first step toward transformation is courage—the courage to start small, persist, and trust in the brain's ability to change.

Organizational Implications: A High-Level View

Just as neuroplasticity enables individuals to reshape their habits and behaviors, organizations have the capacity to rewire their cultures, systems, and ways of working. Much like the brain, organizations develop "pathways"—patterns reinforced by repetition, incentives, and shared beliefs. These pathways dictate how teams collaborate, innovate, and respond to challenges.

Over time, these pathways can become deeply ingrained. While they may have served the organization's goals in the past, they can also lead to stagnation, inefficiency, and resistance to change. Fortunately, the principles of neuroplasticity offer a roadmap for transformation at an organizational level.

The Organizational Brain: Pathways of Culture and Behavior

Think of an organization as a collective brain. Each team, department, and leader represents a neuron, and the connections between them form the organization's pathways. These pathways are shaped by:

- **Repetition:** Practices and behaviors repeated over time become the norm.

- **Reinforcement:** Behaviors that are rewarded or recognized become stronger and more ingrained.

- **Exposure:** The organizational "exposure" to diverse perspectives, cross-functional collaboration, and new experiences accelerates growth and transformation—challenging old assumptions and creating new pathways for innovation.

Example: Siloed Operations

A global retailer faced inefficiencies due to siloed departments, where each function optimized its own processes but failed to collaborate on company-wide initiatives. This siloed culture had become a well-trodden pathway, reinforced by departmental KPIs that prioritized individual success over collective goals.

To rewire this behavior, the company implemented changes inspired by neuroplasticity:

1. **Repetition:** They introduced cross-functional task forces to work on shared goals, creating opportunities for collaboration.

2. **Reinforcement:** Teams that achieved collaborative milestones were celebrated in company-wide meetings, strengthening the pathway of teamwork.

3. **Reflection:** Post-project debriefs allowed teams to discuss lessons learned, reinforcing the value of collaboration.

Within a year, the company saw measurable improvements in efficiency and innovation, demonstrating how deliberate effort can rewire organizational behaviors.

Looking Ahead: Organizational Neuroplasticity in Action

This chapter has introduced the idea that organizations, like individuals, have pathways that can be rewired. In subsequent chapters, we will explore how these principles apply to specific challenges, such as breaking down silos, fostering collaboration, and building a culture of adaptability.

For now, remember that transformation begins with small, intentional steps. By applying the principles of neuroplasticity, leaders can create environments where teams and organizations thrive.

The science of neuroplasticity is not just a fascinating discovery—it is a practical tool for driving transformation. Whether you are striving to overcome personal barriers, lead a team, or reshape an organization, the principles of neuroplasticity provide a clear roadmap for creating meaningful and lasting change.

Chapter Summary

- **Neuroplasticity is your brain's ability to rewire itself—** forming new pathways through repeated thoughts, actions, and experiences.

- **Old habits are not permanent**; they are simply well-worn neural pathways that can be reshaped with intention and practice.

- The three key drivers of rewiring are:

  - → **Repetition** (consistent practice),

  - → **Reinforcement** (positive feedback and reward), and

  - → **Exposure** (new experiences, perspectives, and environments that challenge default thinking and expand possibilities)

- **Short-term changes** (chemical) give us motivation, but only **long-term repetition** (structural changes) lead to lasting transformation.

- Real-life stories (like Sarah and Priya) illustrate how small daily actions, when repeated, **shift mindset and behavior over time.**

- Neuroplasticity isn't just a personal concept—it's a powerful framework for **organizational change**, shaping how cultures evolve.

Action Exercises

The principles of neuroplasticity are most powerful when applied. These exercises are designed to help you identify areas for growth, create new pathways, and reinforce positive behaviors. Whether focusing on personal habits or workplace challenges, these activities provide a practical starting point for transformation.

1. Rewire a Habit That No Longer Serves You

Every leader has patterns—some empower growth, while others hold them back. Identify one habit that is limiting your effectiveness and start reshaping it.

Step 1: Identify the habit loop (Trigger → Behavior → Reward).

- Example:
  - Trigger: Tight deadlines.
  - Behavior: Micromanaging the team.
  - Reward: Feeling in control but adding stress.

Step 2: Replace the habit with a positive alternative.

- Example: Instead of micromanaging, set clear expectations upfront and schedule a weekly check-in instead of daily involvement.

Step 3: Reinforce the new behavior through consistent action and feedback.

- Track progress by reflecting on how often you let go and empower your team.

2. Strengthen a New Leadership Skill Through Repetition

Mastering a new leadership behavior takes consistent practice—just like training a muscle.

Step 1: Choose a leadership behavior to strengthen.

- Example: Practicing active listening in meetings.

Step 2: Set a clear action plan for daily reinforcement.

- Example: In every conversation, summarize what you heard before responding.

Step 3: Reinforce and track progress.

- Example: Ask a trusted colleague for feedback on how well you're implementing the skill.

3. Break the "Wrong Wiring" in Your Team

Teams develop hard-wired patterns—some productive, others limiting. Identify one team behavior that's blocking progress and begin reshaping it.

Step 1: Observe repeated team behaviors that don't align with goals.

- Example: Team members hesitate to speak up in meetings.

Step 2: Uncover the reason behind the pattern.

- Example: Fear of criticism or feeling unheard.

Step 3: Introduce a small, consistent change to rewire team culture.

- Example: Open every meeting by having each team member share one insight or idea before discussion starts.

4. Reinforce Positive Behaviors with Recognition

What gets recognized and rewarded becomes part of the culture. Use reinforcement to lock in new leadership behaviors.

Step 1: Identify a positive leadership behavior you want to reinforce in your team.

- Example: Cross-functional collaboration.

Step 2: Actively recognize individuals demonstrating this behavior.

- Example: Highlight a great collaboration success story in a team meeting.

Step 3: Embed recognition into leadership rituals.

- Example: Start a weekly "Leadership Spotlight" where peers recognize each other for positive contributions.

5. Share and Multiply Your Growth

Neuroscience proves that transformation spreads when it's shared. Sharing your progress reinforces your own learning and inspires others to grow.

Step 1: Identify one breakthrough or lesson from this chapter.

Step 2: Share it with your team, peers, or mentor.

Step 3: Encourage others to experiment with these insights.

Chapter 2:

Hard Wiring and the Workplace

Walk into any longstanding organization and you'll likely feel it—not just see it. The rhythm of routines, the unspoken rules, the predictable ways of working. There's an invisible script playing out every day: how meetings are run, how decisions get made, who speaks up and who stays quiet.

These patterns, though often efficient, can become invisible barriers to change. What started as smart shortcuts—like approval workflows, performance rituals, or leadership styles—harden into unquestioned defaults over time. These are the organization's **mental highways**, built through repetition and reinforced by success. This is the essence of **organizational hard wiring**.

In Chapter 1, we explored how neuroplasticity shapes the brain—how repeated thoughts and actions build strong neural pathways that become second nature. The same is true for organizations. The culture, systems, and leadership behaviors that are repeated most often become deeply embedded, guiding how people think, act, and collaborate—even when those ways no longer serve the business.

Just like a brain can be rewired, so too can an organization. But only if its people recognize the wiring that's holding them back.

This chapter uncovers how hard wiring forms in the workplace, how it silently shapes behavior, and why it can make transformation so difficult—despite good intentions. You'll learn to spot the signs of deeply embedded patterns, explore how limiting beliefs fuel organizational stagnation, and begin to see how you can shift the underlying beliefs that keep your team, your processes, and your culture stuck.

When Hard Wiring Becomes a Roadblock

Consider a large hospital that prided itself on its reputation for clinical excellence. For years, it relied on handwritten documentation and rigid approval chains for every procedural change. These systems ensured accountability—but as patient volume grew and digital tools emerged, this hard wiring became a bottleneck.

- Nurses spent valuable time filling out paperwork instead of attending to patients.

- Junior doctors hesitated to suggest workflow improvements, fearing pushback from senior staff.

- Attempts to introduce electronic health records (EHRs) were met with resistance, citing "this is how we've always done it."

What once guaranteed safety and consistency now hindered adaptability, collaboration, and innovation. The hospital's deeply entrenched routines—its hard wiring—created a drag on its ability to evolve.

Breaking Free from Outdated Patterns

By understanding the dynamics of hard wiring in the workplace, leaders and teams can take deliberate steps to evolve their culture, challenge outdated patterns, and build an environment ready for transformation.

Reflection for Readers

- What workplace habits or "default settings" feel automatic— even if they no longer serve your goals?

- Are there decision-making processes or team dynamics that could benefit from intentional rewiring?

- Where might your organization be relying on old formulas in a changed world?

The Making of Hard Wiring in Organizations

Imagine a river gradually carving a canyon through rock. With every drop of water following the same path, the groove deepens—until the river cannot easily change course.

That's how organizational hard wiring is formed. Over time, repeated decisions, behaviors, and systems carve deep grooves into how work gets done. What starts as a practical solution—a way to manage growth, ensure quality, or reduce risk—eventually becomes automatic. What once enabled success can later create rigidity.

How Organizational Habits Take Root

In the early stages of growth, companies establish habits to solve immediate problems:

- A **strict approval process** is put in place to maintain quality.

- A **hierarchical decision-making model** ensures control and consistency.

- **Templates and workflows** help standardize practices across regions.

These choices are useful—until they aren't.

Over time, these solutions become invisible norms. People stop questioning whether the process still fits the problem. They follow the path because it's familiar, not because it's optimal.

Key Insight: Organizational habits are not just systems. They are **stories and signals** reinforced through repetition, rewarded behaviors, and unspoken rules. That's what makes them hard to change.

Case Study: From Command to Collaboration

A traditional manufacturing firm had thrived for decades under a command-and-control model. Decision-making was centralized, and employees followed procedures without question. It created consistency—but at the cost of innovation.

When the company embarked on a digital transformation, its hard wiring became a barrier:

- Teams waited for instructions rather than initiating change.

- Managers focused on compliance rather than coaching.

- Innovation efforts stalled due to siloed thinking.

To rewire its culture, leadership took bold steps:

- Decision rights were redistributed to empower local teams.

- Mid-level managers were trained in coaching, not just supervision.

- Cross-functional idea-sharing forums were introduced.

Over time, the culture shifted from *"follow the plan"* to *"own the outcome."* Teams became more confident, agile, and accountable. What changed wasn't just the process—it was the underlying belief system and behavior architecture.

Why Hard Wiring Feels Natural

Repetition strengthens organizational pathways just as it does neural pathways in the brain. Practices that are repeated become "muscle memory" for teams, creating a sense of normalcy. Even when these patterns no longer serve the organization's goals, they feel safe and familiar.

Positive and Negative Examples of Hard Wiring

Hard wiring can show up in both enabling and limiting ways. For instance, an organization might build in weekly learning sessions that reinforce innovation—a positive form of wiring. In contrast, when outdated workflows persist simply because "this is how we've always done it," that's hard wiring working against progress. The key isn't whether wiring exists—it's whether it's aligned with where the organization wants to go.

The Role of Reinforcement

Hard wiring is sustained by reinforcement. Behaviors that are rewarded—formally or informally—become repeated. Sometimes these reinforcements are explicit, like performance reviews or promotions. More often, they are subtle: which voices are listened to in meetings, which risks are applauded, which mistakes are tolerated.

If an employee suggests an idea and gets ignored, that's a form of reinforcement too—teaching them not to speak up next time.

Sustained transformation requires rethinking not just what we encourage, but what we unknowingly reinforce.

Three Steps to Intentional Rewiring: Replacing Outdated Hard Wiring

Just like the brain rewires itself through repetition and reinforcement, organizations can disrupt entrenched patterns and form new, productive pathways. This rewiring doesn't happen by chance—it requires deliberate, repeated action. Here's a simple framework to begin:

Step 1: Identify the Old Loop

What habit, system, or mindset is being repeated but no longer serves your goals?

Example: Teams wait for leader approval on every initiative—even low-risk ones—slowing decision-making and eroding ownership.

Step 2: Define the New Loop

What belief or behavior would serve better? Frame it as a clear, repeatable action.

Example: Teams use a decision rights matrix to make autonomous decisions within defined boundaries.

Step 3: Design for Repetition

Embed the new loop into recurring rituals, systems, or workflows to make it stick.

Example: Weekly team huddles include a "What decision did we make without escalation?" spotlight to normalize empowerment.

This process may feel small, but over time, it rewires the organizational "muscle memory"—moving transformation from intent to instinct.

Reflection for Readers

- What pathways exist in your organization today? Are they aligned with your transformation goals?

- How might you disrupt unproductive patterns to carve new pathways for growth?

Looking Ahead: Later in the book, we'll explore how to redesign these pathways through system-level rewiring—but it begins here, with awareness of what's already hardwired.

Wrong Wiring: Common Workplace Pitfalls

Hard wiring isn't inherently bad—it often serves as the backbone of an organization's operations. However, when these deeply ingrained patterns become misaligned with current goals or external realities, they turn into "wrong wiring." These misaligned pathways can stifle creativity, slow decision-making, and prevent organizations from adapting to change.

Let's examine some of the most common pitfalls caused by wrong wiring and their impact on organizational growth and transformation.

1. Silos: The Walls That Divide

Silos occur when teams or departments prioritize their own objectives over organizational outcomes. Often rooted in structural issues—such as separate KPIs or competing resource allocation—silos are reinforced by cultural barriers like mistrust or poor communication.

Example: Siloed Thinking in a Global Tech Company

At a global tech firm, the marketing, sales, and product teams operated independently, optimizing their own processes without collaborating on shared goals. When the company launched a flagship product, the lack of cross-functional collaboration led to:

- Misaligned messaging that confused customers.
- Delayed rollouts due to duplicated efforts.
- Missed opportunities to create a cohesive customer experience.

Impact:

Silos hinder knowledge-sharing, slow decision-making, and limit an organization's ability to tackle complex challenges that require collaboration. Organizations stuck in silos struggle to adapt and innovate.

2. Resistance to Change

The phrase "this is how we've always done it" encapsulates a mindset of resistance that plagues many organizations. Rooted in fear of the unknown, this wiring blocks progress and prevents organizations from evolving.

Example: A Family-Owned Business's Digital Dilemma

A family-owned retail chain built its reputation on personalized customer service, believing that adopting e-commerce would weaken this connection. While competitors embraced digital transformation, the company clung to traditional in-store interactions, convinced that automation would erode its human touch.

However, as customer preferences shifted online, the company's reluctance to evolve led to:

- Declining market relevance, as shoppers favored the convenience of digital platforms.
- Missed opportunities for growth, while competitors expanded through omnichannel strategies.

Impact:

Resistance to change creates inertia, making it harder for businesses to adapt to external shifts. Over time, stagnation leads to declining competitiveness, shrinking market share, and lost relevance—even for once-thriving brands.

3. The Blame Culture

In a blame culture, mistakes are met with criticism rather than curiosity. This environment discourages risk-taking and stifles innovation, as employees focus on self-preservation rather than progress.

Example: A Retail Organization's Toxic Cycle

A large retail company fostered a punitive management culture, where mistakes were publicly criticized rather than treated as learning opportunities. Over time, this fear-driven environment led to:

- Employees avoiding innovation, hesitant to propose new ideas for fear of being reprimanded.

- A stagnant organization, as risk-taking and creativity were replaced by compliance and self-preservation.

Impact:

Blame destroys trust and psychological safety, two essential pillars of collaboration and innovation. When employees fear repercussions, they stop experimenting, stop contributing, and stop growing—leaving the company vulnerable to disruption from more adaptive competitors.

4. Overdependence on Legacy Systems

Organizations that rely heavily on outdated technologies or processes often struggle to adapt to new demands. While legacy systems may have served well in the past, clinging to them limits scalability and innovation.

Example: A Financial Institution's Bottleneck

A financial services company depended on decades-old software to manage customer accounts. While the system was still functional, it lacked integration with modern digital platforms. Meanwhile, competitors launched seamless mobile banking experiences, leaving the company struggling to keep up. As a result, it faced:

- Inefficiencies in processing customer requests, leading to delays and frustration.

- Difficulty attracting tech-savvy customers, as digital-first banking became the norm.

Impact:

Overreliance on outdated systems creates operational bottlenecks, slows down innovation, and erodes competitiveness. In a fast-evolving financial landscape, failing to modernize not only impacts customer satisfaction but also prevents long-term growth.

The Common Thread: Reinforced Pathways

In each of these pitfalls, wrong wiring becomes self-reinforcing. Behaviors like micromanagement, siloed thinking, and resistance to change persist because they feel familiar and safe, even when they no longer serve the organization's goals. Leaders must recognize that disrupting these patterns requires intentional effort and a willingness to challenge the status quo.

Reflection for Readers

- Can you identify any of these pitfalls in your organization?

- What behaviors, systems, or beliefs might be reinforcing them, and how could they be disrupted?

Looking Ahead: In later chapters, we'll explore how to rewire these deeply embedded behaviors through intentional system design, feedback loops, and leader-led change.

The Role of Limiting Beliefs

At the heart of much organizational hard wiring lies an invisible force: **limiting beliefs**. These are deeply held assumptions—about change, risk, capability, or capacity—that shape how people behave and how decisions are made. They're not always visible, but they form the foundation of patterns that persist, even when they no longer serve the organization's goals.

A belief like *"Failure is unacceptable"* doesn't just affect decisions—it creates a culture of fear that stifles innovation. Similarly, *"Our people aren't ready"* can block investments in learning and development before anyone even tries.

These beliefs often feel like truths, when they're actually inherited narratives—reinforced over time, and rarely questioned.

That's why in the next chapter, we'll go deeper into how limiting beliefs form, how they constrain transformation, and how leaders can surface, challenge, and replace them with more empowering perspectives.

Closing Story: Rewiring from the Ground Up

A mid-sized architecture firm had long operated under a traditional, top-down culture. Leaders made decisions in isolation, junior team members executed without question, and innovation had stalled. The hard wiring ran deep—meetings were one-way, recognition flowed only upward, and initiative was quietly discouraged.

When the firm began losing younger talent to more progressive competitors, leadership realized it wasn't just a retention issue—it was a rewiring issue.

They didn't start with grand strategy. Instead, they introduced a new ritual: weekly design huddles where every team member—regardless of level—could share input on client work. Senior leaders stepped back, listened, and highlighted ideas that came from unexpected places.

Over time, something subtle but powerful shifted. Junior architects began taking more initiative. Collaboration increased across departments. Leaders who once guarded decisions began asking for feedback.

This wasn't about new tools or org charts. It was about challenging the assumptions baked into daily behavior—and creating new patterns that signaled: we trust you. We want your voice. We're building something different.

Rewiring begins with behavior. But it's sustained when beliefs evolve too.

The Road Ahead

Rewiring visible behaviors is a powerful first step—but beneath every ritual, system, and habit lies something deeper: belief. What we normalize, what we resist, what we repeat—all of it is shaped by the assumptions we carry, often without even realizing it.

In the next chapter, we'll explore these hidden forces—limiting beliefs—and how they quietly shape culture, decisions, and resistance to change. Because if hard wiring is the pattern, belief is the blueprint. And transformation becomes truly sustainable when we change not just how we act—but how we think.

Chapter Summary

Hard wiring refers to deeply embedded behaviors, systems, and norms in an organization, formed through repetition and reinforced over time.

While hard wiring provides efficiency and stability, it becomes a liability when misaligned with today's fast-paced, innovation-driven environment.

Four common pitfalls of "wrong wiring" include:

→ Silos,

→ Resistance to change,

→ Blame cultures, and

→ Legacy system dependence.

Reinforcement—what is rewarded, tolerated, or ignored—sustains both good and bad wiring.

To shift from outdated patterns to empowering ones, leaders must:

→ **Identify the Old Loop**: Pinpoint specific behaviors or systems that no longer support your transformation goals.

→ **Define the New Loop**: Clarify the improved behavior or belief you want to embed—make it simple and repeatable.

→ **Design for Repetition**: Build the new behavior into everyday routines, meetings, or rituals so it becomes second nature.

Limiting beliefs (e.g., "Failure is unacceptable") often operate silently, blocking transformation unless surfaced and challenged.

Change begins not with new structures, but by re-examining and reshaping the assumptions and behaviors woven into daily work.

Action Exercises

These exercises are designed to help you identify and begin rewiring entrenched behaviors in your workplace. Whether you are a leader, manager, or team member, these practical steps will guide you in applying the principles from this chapter.

1. Conduct a Team Process Audit

Objective: Identify one routine or process within your team or organization that may be hard-wired but no longer effective.

Steps:

1. Ask these key questions:
   - Why do we do it this way?
   - Is it aligned with our current goals?
   - Are there alternative approaches that could improve outcomes?
2. Involve your team in brainstorming improvements or alternatives.

Action Step: Select one aspect of the process to revise and test a new approach for a set period (e.g., two weeks).

2. Surface Limiting Beliefs

Objective: Identify and challenge beliefs that may be reinforcing unproductive patterns in your organization.

Steps:

- Gather your team and brainstorm limiting beliefs holding the organization back.
  1. Examples: *"We don't have enough resources." / "This is how we've always done it."*
- Discuss how these beliefs shape decisions and behaviors.
- Choose one belief to reframe into an empowering narrative.

1. *Example:*

   - **Limiting Belief:** "Change is too risky."

   - **Reframed Narrative:** "Risk-taking drives innovation and growth."

Action Step: Create an actionable plan based on the reframed belief and implement it over the next 2–4 weeks.

📘 *(We'll explore belief reframing in greater depth in part 2 of the book.)*

3. Start a "What If?" Conversation

Objective: Spark curiosity and encourage teams to question the status quo.

Steps:

1. Dedicate 30 minutes in your next team meeting to explore new possibilities by asking:

   - What if we tried a completely different approach to this challenge?

   - What if we removed this process altogether—how would it affect outcomes?

2. Capture and evaluate ideas for feasibility and impact.

Action Step: Commit to testing one idea that emerges from this discussion.

4. Design and Embed a New Ritual

Objective: Reinforce a transformation mindset by replacing outdated behaviors with intentional, repeatable rituals.

Steps:

- Identify a behavior or mindset you want to cultivate—such as collaboration, innovation, or accountability.

- Brainstorm a ritual that aligns with this goal. Consider both individual and team-based options:

1. Start weekly meetings with a success story that demonstrates cross-functional collaboration.

2. Introduce a "Fail Forward Friday" to share lessons from risks taken.

3. Kick off every Monday with a rotating team member sharing one insight from customer feedback.

Action Step:

Pilot the ritual for four weeks and gather feedback on its emotional and cultural impact.

5. Create a Feedback Loop

- **Objective:** Monitor progress and reinforce new behaviors through consistent feedback.

- **Steps:**

   1. Choose a behavior or process you're trying to change.

   2. Establish a feedback mechanism to track progress, such as:

      - Regular team check-ins to discuss what's working and what's not.

      - Anonymous surveys to gather candid input.

   3. Use feedback to refine and reinforce the desired behavior.

- **Action Step:** Share progress and insights with the team to build momentum and accountability.

Reflection for Readers

- What is one entrenched behavior or belief in your workplace that you want to change?

- Which strategy from this chapter could you implement today to begin rewiring it?

Chapter 3

Challenging Limiting Beliefs: Unlocking New Perspectives

Imagine standing in a vast, open field with endless possibilities ahead of you. Now, imagine wearing heavy chains that prevent you from moving forward freely. These chains represent **limiting beliefs**—deep-seated assumptions and mental narratives that shape our perceptions, decisions, and actions. While they offer a sense of security and familiarity, they also restrict growth, creativity, and transformation. These unspoken assumptions quietly but powerfully shape how individuals, teams, and organizations operate. They act as the foundation for the entrenched hard wiring we explored in Chapter 2, reinforcing patterns that can feel immovable.

While hard wiring manifests in behaviors, limiting beliefs are the architects behind those behaviors. They whisper, "This is how it's always been," or, "That's too risky," ensuring that well-worn pathways are followed, even when they no longer serve the organization's goals. Left unchallenged, limiting beliefs create a false sense of security that stifles creativity, blocks innovation, and narrows opportunities.

In this chapter, we will explore how limiting beliefs take root, how they shape behaviors at both individual and organizational levels, and most importantly, how to identify, challenge, and dismantle them to unlock new potential.

Unlike reframing, which will be explored in Chapter 9, this chapter focuses on recognizing and questioning the fundamental assumptions that hold us back. It is about surfacing these hidden beliefs, examining their impact, and consciously replacing them with more empowering perspectives.

Why Limiting Beliefs Matter in Transformation

Limiting beliefs are not inherently bad—they often originate as protective mechanisms to avoid failure or uncertainty. However, in a rapidly changing world, the beliefs that once provided stability can become barriers to progress. Consider these scenarios:

- A team resists adopting a new technology, believing, "Our people aren't ready." This belief delays critical advancements, allowing competitors to gain an edge.

- A leader avoids risk, convinced that "Failure is unacceptable," stifling experimentation and creativity across the organization.

In each case, these beliefs keep organizations rooted in the past, unable to adapt to evolving realities. For transformation to occur, these narratives must be surfaced, challenged, and replaced with empowering perspectives.

Reflection for Readers

Before diving deeper, take a moment to reflect:

- What beliefs—personal or organizational—might be shaping your decisions today?

- Are these beliefs propelling you forward, or are they acting as barriers to progress?

What Are Limiting Beliefs?

Limiting beliefs are the invisible forces that shape our actions, decisions, and perceptions of what is possible. They act as mental shortcuts, providing a sense of order in a complex world, but they also create psychological and organizational barriers that prevent exploration, innovation, and growth.

At their core, limiting beliefs are assumptions—often subconscious—that individuals and organizations accept as truth.

Types of Limiting Beliefs

1. **Personal Beliefs:** These are individual assumptions about one's capabilities or limitations. For example, an employee might believe, "I'm not creative," which prevents them from contributing innovative ideas.

2. **Team Beliefs:** These are collective narratives that influence group behavior. For example, a team might think, "We can't collaborate with other departments because they don't understand our work," leading to siloed operations.

3. **Organizational Beliefs:** These are systemic assumptions that shape an organization's culture and decision-making. For instance, "Change is too risky" might discourage exploration and experimentation.

4. **Cultural Beliefs:** These are broader societal or industry norms that impact organizational behavior. For example, "Our industry is too traditional for innovation" can limit an organization's ability to disrupt the market.

The Origins of Limiting Beliefs

Understanding the origins of limiting beliefs is essential to breaking free from them. These beliefs often form due to:

1. Past Experiences & Failures

When we encounter setbacks, our brain tends to generalize the experience to protect us from future harm. For example, if a leader once proposed an idea that was rejected, they may develop the belief that "My ideas are not valuable," leading to self-censorship in the future.

2. Social Conditioning & Cultural Norms

Many limiting beliefs are deeply embedded in workplace cultures. Organizations that have historically valued stability over experimentation often reinforce the idea that "Risk is dangerous." Over time, this becomes a self-fulfilling prophecy, discouraging teams from taking bold steps.

3. Authority & Hierarchical Influence

Leaders and mentors play a powerful role in shaping beliefs. If a senior leader constantly emphasizes cost-cutting and short-term efficiency, employees may internalize the belief that "Creativity is a waste of time," preventing long-term strategic thinking.

4. The Brain's Need for Predictability

The human brain prefers certainty and patterns. Limiting beliefs offer a structured way of thinking, reducing cognitive load. However, this preference for stability can make us resistant to unlearning outdated ideas, even when they no longer serve us.

Identifying Your Limiting Beliefs

The first step in challenging limiting beliefs is identifying them. Many of these beliefs operate below the surface, subtly influencing decisions. Use the following prompts to uncover them:

1. The "Why" Challenge

Ask "Why?" multiple times to get to the root of an assumption.

- "We can't try this new approach." → Why?
- "Because it's risky." → Why?
- "Because failure might hurt our reputation." → Why?
- "Because we belleve failure is unacceptable."

2. The "If It Weren't True" Test

Challenge your assumption by imagining a world where the opposite is true:

- Limiting Belief: "Our team lacks creativity."
- What if this weren't true? What would be different?
- What evidence exists that contradicts this belief?

3. The Pattern Recognition Method

Look for recurring patterns in behavior:

- Are decisions being avoided due to fear of failure?

- Are teams defaulting to "business as usual" rather than exploring new approaches?

Challenging and Dismantling Limiting Beliefs

Once we surface limiting beliefs, the next step is **challenging them** to make room for more empowering perspectives.

1. Separate Fact from Interpretation

Many beliefs are interpretations of past experiences, not facts. Ask yourself:

- "Is this belief based on evidence, or is it an assumption?"

- "Has this belief ever been proven wrong?"

2. Seek Counter-Evidence

Look for examples that disprove the limiting belief.

- If a team believes "We can't work cross-functionally," find examples where collaboration was successful, even in small ways.

3. Use Empowering Language

Words shape thoughts. Replacing rigid language with growth-oriented statements can shift mindsets:

- Instead of: "We can't do this."

- Try: "We haven't done this before, but we can explore how."

- Instead of: "Failure is bad."

- Try: "Failure provides valuable learning."

4. Adopt a "Test-and-Learn" Approach

Encourage small experiments to test new behaviors and break the cycle of limiting beliefs.

- Example: If a company believes "Innovation won't work in our industry," run a small pilot project to experiment in a low-risk way.

Final Thoughts: Making the Shift

Limiting beliefs are not immovable barriers—they are mental constructs that can be challenged, reshaped, and replaced with more empowering perspectives. The key to transformation is self-awareness and deliberate action. By questioning assumptions, testing new possibilities, and actively shifting perspectives, individuals and organizations can unlock their full potential and embrace continuous growth.

While challenging limiting beliefs is the first step, sustainable transformation requires more than just removing mental roadblocks—it requires rewiring the way we think, behave, and operate in our environments.

In the next chapter, we will explore how reshaping behaviors and environments reinforces transformation. We'll dive into the neuroscience behind workplace change and examine how small shifts in habits and organizational culture can create lasting impact. By understanding how beliefs translate into daily practices, leaders can drive meaningful change at every level of the organization.

Chapter Summary

- Limiting **beliefs are deep-seated mental assumptions** that shape how individuals and organizations perceive what's possible. Often subconscious, they create invisible barriers that block innovation, adaptability, and growth.

- These beliefs originate from **past experiences, social conditioning, leadership influence**, and the brain's preference for predictability. While they offer a sense of security, they often reinforce outdated behaviors.

- Limiting beliefs operate at multiple levels:

    → **Personal** ("I'm not creative")

    → **Team** ("They won't understand our work")

    → **Organizational** ("Change is too risky")

    → **Cultural** ("This industry doesn't innovate")

- To dismantle limiting beliefs, leaders must first **identify them** using tools like the "Why" challenge, the "What if it weren't true?" test, and pattern recognition.

- Once surfaced, beliefs should be **challenged through evidence, reframing language**, and **low-risk experimentation.**

- Replacing limiting beliefs with empowering ones unlocks energy, creativity, and forward movement—both for individuals and entire organizations.

- True transformation starts by shifting **mindsets**, not just systems. When beliefs change, behavior follows.

Action Exercises

Challenging limiting beliefs requires deliberate practice and action. Awareness alone isn't enough—real transformation happens when individuals and teams actively confront and replace outdated assumptions. The following exercises are designed to help you surface, question, and disrupt limiting beliefs in practical ways, fostering a culture of growth and possibility.

1. Conduct a Belief Audit

- List three beliefs that influence your decisions at work.
- Identify whether each belief is empowering or limiting.
- Challenge one limiting belief by asking, "Is this absolutely true?"

2. The Counter-Evidence Exercise

- Write down a limiting belief.
- Find at least three real-life examples that contradict it.
- Reflect on how this new evidence changes your perspective.

3. The Language Shift Practice

- Identify a common phrase you or your team use that reinforces a limiting belief.
- Replace it with a more growth-oriented statement.
- Practice using this new language in daily conversations.

4. Small Experiment Challenge

- Choose one belief you want to test.
- Design a small, low risk experiment to challenge this belief.
- Observe the outcome and reflect on what you've learned.

5. Reflection Journal

- At the end of each day, write one instance where a limiting belief influenced your decision.

- Consider alternative ways you could have responded.

- Track progress over time to see how your mindset shifts.

Reflection for Readers

- Which of these tools resonates most with your current challenges?

- How can you adapt these exercises to your team or organization?

Chapter 4:

Rewiring the Workplace: Neuroplasticity in Action

In Chapter 3, we explored how limiting beliefs act as invisible barriers, constraining individual and organizational growth. While challenging and reframing these beliefs is a critical step in transformation, true progress requires more than a shift in mindset. It necessitates embedding new behaviors, systems, and cultural norms into the daily fabric of an organization. This process—rewiring the workplace—is both an art and a science, deeply rooted in the principles of neuroplasticity.

Imagine the workplace as a sprawling web of pathways—some well-trodden and deeply entrenched, others faint trails of new behaviors trying to take root. The well-worn trails represent the habits, routines, and systems that have guided the organization for years. While these pathways may have been effective in the past, they often become obstacles when the organization faces new challenges or strives to innovate. To thrive in today's dynamic environment, leaders must guide their organizations in carving new paths, dismantling outdated habits, and fostering behaviors that align with the vision for growth and resilience.

Rewiring the workplace mirrors the process of neuroplasticity in the human brain. Just as neural pathways are formed through repetition and strengthened by reinforcement, organizational pathways are shaped by repeated actions and cultural norms. Similarly, just as unused neural pathways weaken over time, outdated practices and behaviors in organizations can be pruned and replaced with more effective alternatives. This interplay between repetition and reinforcement is key to embedding sustainable change.

Why Rewiring Matters Now

The urgency for workplace rewiring has never been greater. Rapid technological advancements, shifting workforce dynamics, and evolving customer expectations have created an environment where agility and innovation are no longer optional—they are essential. Yet, many organizations remain tethered to systems and processes that were designed for a different era. These outdated pathways not only hinder progress but also erode employee engagement, stifle creativity, and create resistance to change.

Consider a global financial institution known for its rigid adherence to hierarchical decision-making. While this structure ensured consistency in the past, it became a bottleneck in an industry increasingly driven by agility and customer-centric innovation. Employees hesitated to propose bold ideas, fearing rejection or criticism. Leaders, accustomed to centralized control, struggled to delegate effectively. The result was a culture of inertia, with the organization losing market relevance as competitors embraced more adaptive strategies. This institution's story illustrates why workplace rewiring is critical: without it, even the most visionary plans will falter under the weight of outdated systems.

Rewiring: A Leadership Imperative

Workplace rewiring is not a one-size-fits-all solution. It demands thoughtful leadership, tailored strategies, and a deep understanding of the organization's unique dynamics. Leaders play a pivotal role in this process, serving as architects of transformation. Their ability to model new behaviors, challenge entrenched norms, and foster an environment of trust and psychological safety determines whether the rewiring efforts succeed or fail.

Rewiring the workplace also requires empathy. Change is inherently uncomfortable, and employees often cling to familiar patterns as a source of stability. Leaders must approach the process with patience and a commitment to guiding their teams through uncertainty. By combining strategy with empathy, leaders can create the conditions for meaningful and lasting transformation.

What You'll Learn in This Chapter

In this chapter, we delve into the science and practice of workplace rewiring. Drawing from the principles of neuroplasticity and behavioral science, we explore how leaders can reshape organizational pathways to foster innovation, collaboration, and adaptability. You'll discover:

1. **The Science of Workplace Rewiring**: How the principles of neuroplasticity parallel organizational behaviors and systems.

2. **Stories of Workplace Rewiring**: Real-world examples of organizations that successfully broke free from entrenched habits.

3. **Practical Strategies for Rewiring**: Actionable tools and frameworks to guide leaders in embedding sustainable change.

4. **Overcoming Challenges**: Common barriers to workplace rewiring and how to address them with creativity and empathy.

By the end of this chapter, you'll not only understand the mechanics of workplace rewiring but also feel equipped to initiate it in your own organization. True transformation begins with intentional effort—and the courage to carve new paths where none exist.

Reflection for Readers

- What habits, systems, or cultural norms in your workplace feel like well-worn trails?

- Are these pathways aligned with your organization's goals, or do they need to be rewired?

The Science of Workplace Rewiring

To understand how to rewire a workplace, it's essential to revisit the neuroscience that underpins transformation. Neuroplasticity—the brain's ability to form and reorganize neural connections—provides a powerful framework for reshaping organizational behaviors and systems. In the workplace, "neural pathways" manifest as habits, cultural norms, and operational routines that define how work gets done. These pathways, much like those in the brain, are strengthened through repetition and reinforcement.

1. How Neuroplasticity Mirrors Workplace Dynamics

Neuroplasticity operates on two key principles that are directly applicable to organizations:

- **Repetition Strengthens Pathways (Hebbian Plasticity):** The more frequently a behavior or action is repeated, the stronger its associated neural connections become. In organizations, this translates to routines, such as recurring workflows or standardized practices, becoming ingrained through repeated use.

- **Unused Pathways Weaken (Synaptic Pruning):** Pathways that are no longer used begin to fade. Similarly, organizational practices that are phased out lose their influence over time, creating space for new behaviors to take root.

Example: Transitioning from Command-and-Control to Empowerment

A legacy manufacturing company had a deeply ingrained culture of top-down decision-making, where every major decision required senior management approval. While effective during periods of growth, this approach became a bottleneck in a competitive environment requiring agility. Recognizing this, leadership initiated "decision-making sprints," empowering teams to make autonomous choices within defined parameters. Over time, as team-led decisions repeatedly demonstrated success, the organization's culture shifted toward empowerment, mirroring the rewiring process of synaptic pruning and new pathway formation.

2. The Organizational Brain: How Pathways Are Built

Organizations form "neural pathways" through three primary mechanisms:

- **Behavioral Patterns:** Repeated actions—such as how meetings are conducted or how feedback is given—create expectations and habits.

- **Cultural Norms:** Shared beliefs and values influence behaviors, shaping how teams interact and make decisions.

- **Operational Systems:** Processes, technologies, and workflows establish the "rules" for how work gets done.

Example: Innovation Pathways in a Startup A tech startup that prioritized weekly brainstorming sessions and rapid prototyping developed a cultural pathway of innovation. Over time, these behaviors became second nature, enabling the organization to pivot quickly and maintain a competitive edge. Conversely, a compliance-heavy public-sector organization that relied on multi-layered approval processes created a pathway of bureaucracy, where even minor decisions required extensive review, stifling efficiency and adaptability.

3. The Role of Reinforcement in Rewiring

Reinforcement is critical to embedding new behaviors and practices. Organizations, like brains, reinforce pathways through feedback, rewards, and recognition. Positive reinforcement strengthens desirable behaviors, while the absence of reinforcement allows unproductive behaviors to persist.

Positive Reinforcement:

- A retail chain transitioning to a customer-first model rewarded frontline employees for consistently delivering exceptional service. Recognizing and celebrating these behaviors helped embed customer-centricity into the organization's DNA.

Negative Reinforcement:

- A blame-heavy workplace culture penalized employees for mistakes, reinforcing a pathway of fear and avoidance. Employees avoided taking risks or proposing new ideas, perpetuating a culture of stagnation.

Reflection for Readers

- What pathways in your organization are currently being reinforced—intentionally or unintentionally?

- Are these pathways aligned with your transformation goals?

4. Why Workplace Rewiring Matters

Without deliberate efforts to rewire, organizations risk becoming stuck in outdated patterns that no longer serve their goals. This misalignment leads to inefficiencies, disengaged employees, and lost opportunities for growth. By applying the principles of neuroplasticity, leaders can create new pathways that foster innovation, adaptability, and collaboration.

Case Study: Shifting Priorities in a Financial Institution A global financial institution known for its risk-averse culture faced declining innovation metrics. Leadership launched a strategic initiative to rewire the organization's mindset by introducing "innovation catalysts"—cross-functional teams tasked with piloting bold ideas. The institution reinforced these efforts through storytelling, sharing success stories of small wins across the organization. Over two years, the innovation metrics improved significantly, and the organization regained its competitive edge.

Key Takeaways

1. **Repetition Builds Habits:** Repeated behaviors form pathways that become the foundation of an organization's culture.

2. **Reinforcement Strengthens Pathways:** Feedback and rewards ensure that desired behaviors become embedded.

3. **Pruning is Essential:** Letting go of outdated practices creates space for innovation and growth.

4. **Rewiring Requires Intentionality:** Leaders must actively design and reinforce pathways that align with the organization's vision.

Stories of Workplace Rewiring

Real-world examples provide powerful insights into how deliberate actions can transform deeply ingrained organizational behaviors and systems. These stories illustrate how leaders can successfully rewire workplace dynamics to foster innovation, collaboration, and adaptability. Let's explore these case studies of transformation.

From Micromanagement to Empowerment

The Challenge: A mid-sized logistics firm had a deeply entrenched culture of micromanagement. Leaders believed that tight control was essential for quality and consistency, creating a dependency loop where employees hesitated to make decisions without approval. This approach stifled creativity, reduced efficiency, and demoralized employees.

Actions Taken: The CEO recognized the need for change and launched a "trust-building initiative" to foster delegation and accountability:

- **Leadership Workshops:** Managers attended sessions on effective delegation and trust-building, learning to empower rather than control their teams.

- **Pilot Projects:** Teams were given autonomy to lead projects without micromanagement.

- **Celebrating Success:** Leadership publicly recognized successful team-led projects, showcasing the benefits of autonomy.

The Outcome: Within 18 months, the firm reported:

- A 25% increase in employee satisfaction.

- Noticeable improvements in innovation, with employees proactively suggesting and implementing process improvements.

- Managers who reported feeling less overwhelmed and more focused on strategic priorities.

Breaking Down Silos in a Global Corporation

The Challenge: A multinational consumer goods company struggled with siloed operations. Departments like marketing, product development, and operations focused on their individual objectives, resulting in misaligned priorities and inefficiencies. Collaboration was limited, and cross-functional projects frequently stalled due to competing goals.

Actions Taken: The company launched a series of cross-functional "innovation sprints" designed to foster collaboration:

- **Collaborative Challenges:** Employees from multiple departments were brought together to solve specific organizational problems.

- **Leadership Participation:** Senior leaders modeled collaboration by actively participating in these sessions.

- **Public Recognition:** Successful cross-functional initiatives were celebrated through company-wide communications, reinforcing the importance of collaboration.

The Outcome: Over two years, the company achieved:

- A 20% improvement in project delivery times.

- Increased employee engagement and morale, as employees experienced the benefits of collaboration.

- Improved customer satisfaction metrics, driven by more cohesive product launches and services.

Reframing Failure as a Growth Opportunity

The Challenge: In a manufacturing company, failure was viewed as unacceptable. Employees avoided experimentation and innovation, fearing harsh repercussions for mistakes. This created a risk-averse culture where incremental improvements replaced bold ideas.

Actions Taken: A newly appointed COO introduced "failure forums" to change the organization's narrative around mistakes:

- **Open Discussions:** Teams analyzed failures openly without fear of judgment, focusing on the lessons learned.

- **Leadership Stories:** Executives shared personal stories of failure and growth to normalize mistakes as part of innovation.

- **Recognition Programs:** Teams that demonstrated resilience and creativity in overcoming setbacks were publicly recognized.

The Outcome: Within three years, the company became an industry leader in innovation, launching multiple new products inspired by lessons learned from prior failures. Employee surveys showed significant increases in engagement and psychological safety.

Cultivating Inclusion in a Tech Startup

The Challenge: A fast-growing tech startup struggled with a lack of diversity and inclusion, leading to homogeneity in thought and creativity. This dynamic limited innovation and alienated potential hires from underrepresented groups.

Actions Taken: The CEO spearheaded a comprehensive effort to create a more inclusive culture:

- **Bias Training:** Leadership and hiring managers participated in workshops on unconscious bias.

- **Redesigned Recruitment:** Job descriptions and hiring processes were restructured to attract diverse candidates.

- **Inclusion Forums:** Regular forums were held to discuss challenges and share ideas for fostering inclusion.

The Outcome: Within two years, the company achieved:

- A 30% increase in diversity in leadership roles.

- Improved employee satisfaction, particularly among underrepresented groups.

- Enhanced problem-solving and innovation driven by diverse perspectives.

5. Transitioning to Agile Practices

The Challenge: A traditional insurance company faced market disruption due to its reliance on rigid workflows and hierarchical decision-making. Competitors using agile methodologies outpaced the company in launching new products and services.

Actions Taken: Leadership spearheaded an agile transformation to improve responsiveness and efficiency:

- **Autonomous Teams:** Teams were restructured to operate independently, with clear ownership of projects.

- **Daily Stand-Ups:** Short, focused meetings became a daily ritual to align teams and remove roadblocks.

- **Feedback Loops:** Regular retrospectives enabled teams to identify and address challenges, fostering continuous improvement.

The Outcome: Within a year, the company achieved:

- A 40% reduction in product development cycles.

- Increased customer satisfaction, as the organization delivered faster, more tailored solutions.

- Greater employee engagement, as teams felt empowered to take ownership of their work.

Key Lessons from Workplace Rewiring

1. **Start Small:** Pilot initiatives to demonstrate success before scaling them organization-wide.

2. **Align Changes with Culture:** Ensure that new behaviors and practices resonate with the organization's values and mission.

3. **Celebrate Progress:** Publicly recognize and reward teams or individuals who model the desired behaviors.

4. **Sustain Momentum:** Reinforce new pathways through consistent repetition and feedback.

Reflection for Readers

- Which of these stories resonates most with your organization's challenges?

- What specific steps could you take to apply similar strategies in your workplace?

Practical Strategies for Rewiring the Workplace

Rewiring an organization is a continuous, strategic effort, not a one-time event. While individual behaviors play a role in shaping workplace culture, true transformation is sustained by structural shifts in leadership, decision-making, operational frameworks, and workplace environments.

The detailed discussion on how behavior change and reinforcement shape workplace transformation is covered in Chapter 10: Design –

Building Behavioral Change. This section focuses on the organizational-level changes that support and sustain long-term transformation.

To create a workplace that fosters agility, collaboration, and innovation, organizations must align systems, leadership structures, and workplace environments with transformation goals. Below are key systemic strategies:

1. Leadership Alignment and Distributed Decision-Making

Traditional hierarchical models often slow transformation efforts. Organizations must shift from top-down leadership models to distributed decision-making, where ownership of change is shared across functions.

- Example: A global tech firm transitioned from rigid executive-led approvals to cross-functional leadership teams, allowing for faster, more collaborative decision-making.

- Action: Identify bottlenecks in decision-making and empower mid-level managers to drive transformation initiatives.

2. Rethinking Workspaces to Foster Collaboration

The physical and digital environments in which employees work significantly influence behaviors. A well-designed workspace can reinforce agility, open communication, and knowledge-sharing.

- Example: A financial services company redesigned its office layout with innovation hubs and shared spaces, accelerating cross-functional collaboration.

- Action: Assess whether your workplace layout or digital workspace tools support or hinder collaboration and adaptability.

3. Embedding Transformation in Organizational Rituals

Workplace rituals—such as meetings, reporting structures, and feedback loops—act as reinforcers of organizational norms. Changing these structures can create momentum for transformation.

- Example: A healthcare organization introduced monthly transformation roundtables, where employees shared examples of process improvements they had implemented.

- Action: Replace outdated status meetings with forums focused on learning, experimentation, and transformation updates.

4. Measuring Transformation Progress with New Metrics

Many transformation efforts fail because performance metrics remain unchanged, reinforcing old behaviors and priorities. Organizations must redefine what success looks like in a transformed workplace.

- Example: A retail company moved away from individual sales quotas and began tracking customer lifetime value (CLV) as a team-based metric, fostering collaboration between sales, marketing, and service teams.

- Action: Identify existing KPIs that reinforce outdated behaviors and replace them with metrics aligned with long-term transformation objectives.

5. Systematic Change Through Technology Adoption

Technology should not just automate existing processes—it should be integrated into the transformation strategy to encourage new ways of working.

- Example: A logistics company transitioned to real-time analytics dashboards, shifting from reactive problem-solving to proactive, data-driven decision-making.

- Action: Evaluate whether existing technology investments are enabling transformation or just digitizing outdated processes.

Key Takeaways

- Focus on systemic change, not just behavior shifts.

- Empower leadership at all levels to accelerate decision-making.

- Redesign physical and digital workspaces to foster collaboration.

- Shift KPIs and success metrics to reinforce transformation.

- Use technology strategically to enable, not just automate, change.

By focusing on organizational rewiring, rather than just individual behavior change, leaders can create lasting transformation that is embedded in workplace structures and systems.

Reflection for Readers

- Which of these strategies could you implement in your organization today?

- How might small changes create momentum for larger transformations?

Overcoming Challenges in Rewiring the Workplace

Rewiring a workplace for transformation is inherently challenging. Change disrupts established workflows, decision-making structures, and ingrained organizational habits. Often, resistance emerges not because individuals don't want to change, but because the systems around them make change difficult.

While systemic challenges—such as leadership misalignment, resource constraints, and process inefficiencies—can derail transformation efforts, they are not insurmountable. By addressing these barriers at an organizational level, leaders can build trust, alignment, and momentum for lasting transformation.

For challenges related to individual behavioral resistance and habit formation, see **Chapter 10: Design – Building Behavioral Change.**

1. Skepticism: "Will This Really Work?"

Challenge:

Employees may doubt new transformation efforts, particularly if previous initiatives failed or lacked follow-through.

Systemic Issue:

Organizations often fail to align transformation efforts with existing workflows, making changes feel temporary or disconnected from business priorities.

How to Address It:

- **Align change efforts with business objectives**—Ensure transformation is clearly linked to strategic goals.

- **Show early wins through system-wide pilots**—Start with small, high-impact shifts in key processes.

- **Involve key stakeholders early**—Co-creation fosters credibility and engagement.

Example:

A marketing agency transitioning to agile workflows faced skepticism from senior staff. By running a pilot program in one department, they improved project delivery times by 25%. Sharing this success helped build momentum for broader implementation.

2. Resistance: "This Feels Uncomfortable"

Challenge:

Employees resist change when new structures conflict with ingrained workflows, team dynamics, or reporting hierarchies.

Systemic Issue:

Many organizations fail to redesign workplace systems to support transformation, leading to friction.

How to Address It:

- **Redesign workflows to align with new objectives**—Ensure processes, incentives, and decision-making structures support transformation.

- **Clarify roles & responsibilities in the new model**—Ambiguity creates resistance.

- **Train leaders to support the transition**—Leadership should reinforce the new way of working.

Example:

A manufacturing firm undergoing a digital transformation encountered resistance from long-tenured employees. Leadership provided structured training programs and assigned "digital champions" to mentor teams. Over time, confidence in the new tools increased, reducing resistance.

3. Resource Constraints: "We Don't Have Enough"

Challenge:

Transformation initiatives often face budget limitations, talent shortages, or a lack of executive buy-in.

Systemic Issue:

Many organizations expect transformation without restructuring existing priorities, budgets, or workflows.

How to Address It:

- **Start with low-cost, high-impact changes**—Small operational shifts can drive large-scale impact.

- **Leverage existing tools instead of seeking new investments**—Optimize current technology and processes before adding new ones.

- **Reallocate internal resources strategically**—Align funding and staffing with transformation goals.

Example:

A nonprofit struggling to implement data analytics lacked budget for sophisticated tools. Instead of abandoning the initiative, they partnered with a local university, gaining access to cost-effective solutions that significantly improved donor engagement.

4. Leadership Misalignment: "We're Not All on the Same Page"

Challenge:

Transformation stalls when leaders send mixed messages or fail to model the behaviors and priorities required for change.

Systemic Issue:

Many organizations implement transformation top-down but fail to align leadership at all levels.

How to Address It:

- **Establish a clear, shared vision**—Leaders must consistently communicate the transformation narrative.

- **Model the expected changes**—Executives and mid-level managers must embody the transformation goals.

- **Create accountability mechanisms**—Track and measure leaders' participation in driving change.

Example:

A healthcare organization transitioning to team-based care struggled with conflicting directives from leadership. After hosting an executive retreat to align messaging and expectations, the company successfully accelerated its transformation.

5. Change Fatigue: "We've Tried This Before"

Challenge:

Employees disengage when they feel overwhelmed by continuous transformation efforts.

Systemic Issue:

Organizations often introduce multiple overlapping change initiatives without prioritization or sequencing.

How to Address It:

- **Prioritize & phase transformation initiatives**—Break transformation into manageable steps over time rather than launching multiple initiatives simultaneously.

- **Celebrate milestones to reinforce progress**—Acknowledging incremental success maintains motivation.

- **Balance stability with innovation**—Ensure continuity in core processes while implementing change.

Example:

A retail company shifting to omnichannel sales faced staff burnout. Leadership phased the rollout into manageable stages and celebrated early wins, ensuring sustained engagement.

Key Lessons for Overcoming Challenges

1. **Listen First:** Understand the concerns and fears driving resistance or skepticism.

2. **Lead with Empathy:** Acknowledge the discomfort of change and offer support throughout the process.

3. **Adapt to Feedback:** Use employee input to refine strategies and address barriers in real time.

4. **Maintain Momentum:** Balance quick wins with long-term goals to sustain energy and engagement.

Reflection for Readers

- Which of these challenges resonates most with your organization?

- What steps could you take today to address resistance, skepticism, or resource constraints?

Conclusion: Rewiring the Workplace for Sustainable Change

Rewiring the workplace is both a challenge and an opportunity. It requires leaders to confront entrenched processes, redesign systems, and create structures that support agility and innovation. When transformation is built into the organization's DNA—through leadership alignment, decision-making frameworks, and system-wide shifts—it moves beyond temporary initiatives and becomes a sustainable, scalable strategy.

Transformation is not a linear journey; it demands strategic planning, process evolution, and leadership commitment. While the effort may feel daunting, the rewards are immense: a culture where teams collaborate seamlessly, organizations pivot with agility, and innovation becomes a natural outcome of well-designed systems.

What True Rewiring Looks Like

A **rewired workplace** is one where:

1. Adaptability is Embedded – Decision-making is decentralized, and teams can pivot seamlessly to address challenges and opportunities.

2. Collaboration is Systemic – Siloed operations give way to cross-functional alignment and strategic knowledge-sharing.

3. Innovation is Structured – Organizations implement repeatable mechanisms for testing, scaling, and embedding new ideas.

4. Sustainability is Built In – New ways of working are codified in policies, incentives, and decision frameworks to ensure long-term impact.

A Call to Action

Leaders, the opportunity is in your hands. By understanding the systemic patterns that define your organization, fostering curiosity, and redesigning structures to support continuous transformation, you can create a workplace that is not just reactive but future-ready.

As we transition to the next chapter, we'll explore how rewired systems and transformation strategies can be scaled across teams and functions. The journey does not stop with individual workplaces—it extends to enterprise-wide transformation that ensures adaptability, resilience, and sustainable success.

Reflection for Readers

- What small step can you take today to begin rewiring a practice or behavior in your workplace?

- How can you apply the lessons from this chapter to sustain meaningful change?

Chapter Summary

- **Rewiring the workplace** is the process of intentionally reshaping systems, behaviors, and cultural norms to align with an organization's evolving goals—rooted in the science of neuroplasticity.

- Like the brain, organizations form pathways through **repetition and reinforcement**. These pathways include habitual behaviors, operational systems, and cultural norms that define how work gets done.

- **Reinforcement—what is rewarded, tolerated, or ignored—either sustains outdated habits or strengthens new, productive behaviors.**

- Rewiring efforts are most effective when led by **empathetic, adaptive leaders** who guide change with both strategy and human understanding.

- The chapter highlights **real-world case studies** of transformation—from breaking silos and reframing failure to inclusive culture building and adopting agile practices.

- Organizational rewiring must go beyond individual change. It requires shifts in:

  - **Leadership alignment** and distributed decision-making

  - **Workplace design** to support collaboration

  - **Rituals and metrics** that reinforce new priorities

  - **Technology adoption** that enables, not just digitizes, change

- Common barriers such as skepticism, resistance, change fatigue, and leadership misalignment must be addressed **systemically** to sustain transformation.

- A truly rewired workplace is **agile, collaborative, innovative, and built for sustainable success**—where transformation is no longer a one-time initiative but a way of operating.

Action Exercises

These exercises are designed to help you apply the principles of workplace rewiring in your organization by focusing on structural, leadership, and operational shifts. Start small, iterate, and scale as you build momentum.

1. Spot the "Wrong Wiring" in Organizational Systems

Objective: Identify a workflow, policy, or process that reinforces outdated ways of working.

Steps:

- Review decision-making structures, approval processes, and reporting lines—where are delays or inefficiencies?

- Identify one outdated system that slows innovation or collaboration.

- Propose an alternative structural adjustment, such as simplifying approvals or shifting decision-making authority to frontline teams.

Action Step: Pilot the new workflow for a two-week trial period and track its impact.

2. Rethink Decision-Making Models

Objective: Shift from hierarchical decision-making to a distributed or collaborative model.

Steps:

- Identify key bottlenecks in current decision-making structures.

- Experiment with cross-functional decision-making panels or empowered team leads for small projects.

- Gather feedback on how faster, decentralized decision-making affects efficiency and engagement.

Action Step: Document before-and-after decision timelines and present the findings to leadership for scaling.

3. Transform Workplace Rituals into Systematic Change Enablers

Objective: Rewire organizational habits and meetings to reinforce transformation priorities.

Steps:

- Audit standing meetings, feedback loops, and progress reviews—do they reinforce agility or bureaucracy?

- Design new organizational rituals, such as:

  - Monthly "Rewiring Roundtables" where leaders share process improvements.

  - "Future Focus Fridays" where teams review upcoming challenges collaboratively.

- Remove or streamline legacy rituals that slow down decision-making.

Action Step: Implement one new ritual for a three-month period and assess its impact on efficiency.

4. Align KPIs & Incentives with Workplace Rewiring Goals

Objective: Ensure that success metrics and incentives reinforce new ways of working.

Steps:

- Identify metrics that reinforce outdated behaviors (e.g., measuring individual performance over team outcomes).

- Propose new KPIs, such as:

  - Cross-functional collaboration metrics instead of departmental silos.

  - Customer-centric impact measures rather than internal process adherence.

- Align leadership incentives with rewiring objectives, ensuring that they model the transformation.

Action Step: Pilot new KPIs within one department and assess their impact before organization-wide implementation.

5. Overcome Resistance to Structural Change

Objective: Address systemic resistance to transformation by fostering transparency and co-creation.

Steps:

- Identify a structural change initiative that is facing pushback.

- Conduct cross-functional workshops to surface concerns and collaboratively design improvements.

- Adjust the transformation strategy based on real-time feedback from employees.

Action Step: Implement one change suggested by employees and track engagement levels post-implementation.

6. Prepare the Organization for Enterprise-Wide Scaling

Objective: Move from isolated pilot projects to scalable transformation frameworks.

Steps:

- Identify one successful rewiring initiative that can be scaled across departments.

- Develop a scaling roadmap that includes training, process adjustments, and cross-team collaboration.

- Secure executive sponsorship to integrate changes into company-wide policies.

Action Step: Implement the first scaling phase within three months, with checkpoints for adaptation.

Reflection for Readers

- Which exercise feels most relevant to your organization's current challenges?

- How can these exercises help you begin rewiring unproductive pathways today?

Chapter 5

The Building Blocks of a Transformation Mindset

Transformation is not a one-time effort—it's a sustained way of thinking, acting, and leading. As we've explored in earlier chapters, rewiring beliefs and behaviors through the principles of neuroplasticity lays the foundation for lasting change. But what exactly do we wire ourselves toward?

The answer lies in four essential traits that underpin a transformation-ready mindset: **curiosity**, **adaptability**, **resilience**, and **empowerment**. These are not abstract ideals—they are practiced behaviors that shape how individuals and teams respond to disruption, complexity, and opportunity.

Imagine navigating a maze. For some, the dead ends are signs to retreat. For others, they're prompts to reflect, recalibrate, and keep moving. That difference isn't about tools—it's about mindset. In organizations, the same pattern applies. A transformation mindset doesn't eliminate roadblocks—but it rewires the response to them.

This chapter offers practical guidance, examples, and tools for cultivating these four traits—individually and collectively. By intentionally reinforcing them in daily routines, leadership behaviors, and team interactions, organizations can move from mindset to momentum—and from individual transformation to cultural change.

Reflection for Readers:

- How does your mindset influence the way you approach change, both personally and professionally?

- Which of the four traits—adaptability, curiosity, resilience, or empowerment—does your organization currently exhibit, and which requires further development?

Why Mindset is Central to Transformation

Transformation efforts often falter not because of flawed strategies or insufficient resources, but because they fail to address the human element: mindset. At its core, transformation is a human endeavor, driven by the beliefs, attitudes, and behaviors of individuals and teams. While traditional tools like process optimization, technology upgrades, and strategic realignments address structural and procedural aspects of change, they rarely consider the cultural and psychological factors that ultimately determine success.

The Role of Mindset in Organizational Change

Organizations are not static entities; they are ecosystems of people, each bringing unique perspectives, experiences, and attitudes to their work. These collective mindsets form the bedrock of an organization's culture, shaping how teams respond to challenges, opportunities, and each other.

- **A Fixed Mindset:** This fosters resistance to change and an over-reliance on established practices, even when they no longer serve the organization's goals. It stifles innovation and creates an environment where risk-taking feels unsafe.

- **A Growth-Oriented Mindset:** This encourages openness to new ideas, collaboration, and experimentation. It cultivates a culture where failure is viewed as a stepping stone to success rather than a dead end.

Example: Mindset as a Catalyst for Innovation

A mid-sized healthcare company faced a daunting challenge: its services were rapidly losing relevance as competitors adopted advanced, patient-centric solutions. Initially, the organization clung to a fixed mindset, equating risk with failure. By reframing risk-taking as a learning opportunity, the company unlocked a wave of innovation.

Leadership encouraged cross-functional collaboration, piloted small-scale experiments, and celebrated lessons learned from setbacks. Within three years, the company launched groundbreaking services that improved patient outcomes and significantly boosted revenue.

Why Mindset Matters in Transformation

1. **Mindset Shapes Behavior:** How individuals and teams respond to change is a direct reflection of their mindset. A team that views disruption as an opportunity will approach challenges creatively and decisively, while one that sees it as a threat will retreat into safe, predictable patterns.

2. **Mindset Drives Culture:** The collective mindset influences the values and behaviors that define an organization's culture. A transformation mindset creates a culture of possibility, where adaptability, curiosity, resilience, and empowerment are embedded in daily operations.

3. **Mindset Sustains Change:** Strategies and tools may initiate transformation, but only a growth-oriented mindset sustains it. By keeping teams motivated, aligned, and open to learning, this mindset ensures that change becomes a continuous process rather than a one-time event.

Reflection for Readers

- How does the mindset of your team or organization influence its ability to adapt and innovate?

- Are there fixed mindsets that may be limiting your potential for growth?

The Traits of a Transformation Mindset

Cultivating a transformation mindset is about more than adopting new tools or techniques—it's about embracing attitudes and behaviors that empower individuals and organizations to adapt, innovate, and thrive. Through research and practice, four foundational traits have emerged: adaptability, curiosity, resilience, and empowerment. These traits are not static or innate; they can be developed, strengthened, and embedded into the culture of any organization.

1. Adaptability: Thriving Amid Change

Adaptability is the ability to adjust to new circumstances, pivot in the face of challenges, and embrace change with confidence. In a world where disruption is constant, adaptability is more than a survival skill—it's a competitive advantage.

Story: Adapting to Digital Disruption A global publishing house, once a leader in traditional print media, faced plummeting sales as readers moved to digital platforms. Leadership recognized that clinging to the old model would ensure obsolescence. They embraced adaptability by:

- Restructuring workflows to prioritize digital-first content creation.

- Investing in upskilling employees for digital roles.

- Partnering with tech companies to innovate distribution models.

Within five years, the company transformed into a digital publishing leader, doubling its market share and setting industry benchmarks for innovation.

Practical Strategies to Cultivate Adaptability:

1. **Model Openness to Change:** Leaders should demonstrate flexibility in decision-making and openly embrace new ideas, even if they feel uncertain.

2. **Pilot Small-Scale Experiments:** Encourage teams to test ideas in low-risk environments, gather feedback, and iterate.

3. **Celebrate Adaptive Behaviors:** Publicly recognize individuals and teams who successfully pivot or innovate during times of change.

2. Curiosity: Fuelling Exploration and Learning

Curiosity drives individuals to ask questions, seek new knowledge, and challenge the status quo. It is the foundation of innovation, fostering a culture where exploration, creativity, and experimentation thrive.

Example: The Role of Curiosity in Breakthroughs A leading biotech firm cultivated a culture of curiosity by encouraging researchers to pursue unconventional ideas. One team's willingness to explore a previously overlooked compound led to the discovery of a treatment for a rare disease, generating millions in revenue and saving countless lives.

Practical Exercises to Encourage Curiosity:

1. **Host "What If?" Sessions:** Create safe spaces where teams brainstorm bold ideas without fear of judgment.

2. **Facilitate Cross-Functional Collaboration:** Encourage employees to work across departments, exposing them to diverse perspectives and challenges.

3. **Promote Lifelong Learning:** Offer resources and incentives for continuous education, such as workshops, online courses, or industry conferences.

3. Resilience: Turning Setbacks into Stepping Stones

Resilience is the ability to recover from adversity, persist through challenges, and maintain focus on long-term goals. In transformation, resilience is critical for sustaining momentum amid uncertainty and setbacks.

Story: Bouncing Back from a Setback A retail chain faced significant financial losses when a new product line failed. Instead of retreating, leadership used the setback as an opportunity to learn:

- Teams analyzed what went wrong and documented lessons learned.

- Insights were applied to future product launches, refining development and marketing strategies.

Within two years, the company introduced a series of best-selling products, regaining its market position and building a reputation for innovation.

Strategies to Build Resilience:

1. **Reframe Failure:** Position setbacks as opportunities for growth rather than evidence of incompetence.

2. **Create Psychological Safety:** Foster an environment where employees feel safe to take risks and share vulnerabilities without fear of judgment.

3. **Celebrate Perseverance:** Recognize individuals and teams who demonstrate persistence and creativity in overcoming challenges.

4. Empowerment: Enabling Others to Lead

Empowerment is about giving individuals the autonomy, tools, and confidence to make decisions and take ownership. It transforms employees from passive participants into active drivers of change.

Case Study: Empowerment in Action A logistics company transitioning to digital-first operations decentralized decision-making, giving frontline managers greater autonomy to lead technology adoption. This empowered employees to:

- Accelerate the implementation of new tools.

- Improve operational efficiency by tailoring solutions to on-the-ground needs.

- Boost morale, as employees felt a stronger sense of ownership and purpose.

Tips to Foster Empowerment:

1. **Delegate Meaningfully:** Assign responsibilities that align with employees' strengths and provide opportunities for growth.

2. **Provide Resources and Training:** Equip teams with the tools, knowledge, and support they need to succeed.

3. **Recognize Contributions:** Publicly celebrate the impact of empowered individuals and teams to reinforce confidence and motivation.

Reflection for Readers

- Which of these traits resonates most with your personal leadership style?

- How might you cultivate these traits in your team or organization?

Practical Foundations: Cultivating the Transformation Mindset

Developing a transformation mindset isn't a checklist or a quick fix—it's a deliberate process of cultivating behaviors and attitudes that prepare individuals and organizations to thrive in uncertainty. The traits of adaptability, curiosity, resilience, and empowerment are not just abstract ideals; they are building blocks for creating readiness at every level of the organization.

Connecting Traits to Transformation Readiness

Each of these traits plays a distinct role in fostering a culture capable of transformation:

- **Adaptability** allows teams to navigate shifting priorities and seize emerging opportunities.

- **Curiosity** sparks innovation and challenges assumptions.

- **Resilience** sustains momentum through setbacks and change fatigue.

- **Empowerment** ensures that ownership and leadership are distributed, unlocking untapped potential across the organization.

These traits are the foundation upon which systemic transformation is built, and in Part 2 of this book, we will explore how to embed them into structured systems, processes, and practices through the Catalyst Framework.

Traits in Action: Laying the Groundwork for Transformation

It's one thing to define traits like **curiosity, adaptability, resilience,** and **empowerment**—but it's in action that they gain real power. When these traits are lived out in day-to-day leadership, they become the foundation of a transformation-ready culture. Let's explore how each of these traits shows up meaningfully in practice.

Adaptability: Navigating the Unknown

In Action: Adaptability isn't about reacting quickly—it's about adjusting with intention. It means staying open, revising assumptions, and navigating ambiguity without losing direction.

Real-World Example: A global logistics company had been using the same route optimization algorithm for over a decade. When disruptions during a global supply chain crisis rendered the system ineffective, adaptable leaders empowered their teams to co-create agile workarounds. By creating "what-if scenario" squads, they redesigned workflows in real-time—cutting delivery times by 15% despite the volatility.

Curiosity

In Action: A transformation leader doesn't just ask "What's wrong?"—they ask "What's possible?" Curiosity in action means actively seeking diverse perspectives, encouraging experimentation, and creating space for exploration without fear of failure.

Real-World Example: A technology company facing declining engagement didn't assume it understood the problem. Instead, the leadership team launched a "Listening Lab" initiative—short weekly sessions where employees shared what wasn't working. What emerged was not a technology issue, but a trust gap. This open, curious posture led to new feedback channels, team-led change initiatives, and ultimately, a 20% increase in engagement scores.

Resilience: Bouncing Back Stronger

In Action: Resilience shows up not just in recovery, but in learning. Leaders demonstrate resilience when they absorb setbacks, reflect openly, and use failures as fuel for evolution.

Real-World Example: In the aftermath of a failed product launch, a mid-sized consumer brand didn't hide the setback—it studied it. The CMO hosted an open "Failure Debrief" where teams reviewed the launch timeline, customer feedback, and missed signals. This transparent process uncovered systemic misalignments in product development. Six months later, the brand launched a new product line co-designed with customers and broke previous sales records.

Empowerment: Distributing Leadership

In Action: Empowered leaders don't just delegate—they equip. They transfer ownership, build capability, and provide the safety net needed for others to step up.

Real-World Example: A public sector organization introduced a policy requiring frontline managers to approve new digital service features. Instead of bottlenecking innovation, leaders flipped the model: they trained customer service teams to propose ideas and granted them authority to run pilots. The result? Over 50 service enhancements were implemented in a single year, many of which came from frontline staff closest to the customer.

Preparing for Systemic Transformation

While these traits can drive immediate impact, their full potential is realized when they are embedded into the fabric of an organization. This requires intentional systems, rituals, and practices that reinforce and scale these behaviors. For example:

- Rituals like weekly reflection sessions can sustain resilience.

- Tools like internal knowledge-sharing platforms can foster curiosity.

- Clear delegation frameworks can enhance empowerment.

In **Part 2**, we'll explore how these principles come to life through the Catalyst Framework, providing actionable steps to embed them into your organization's DNA. For now, consider these traits as the groundwork for transformation—essential behaviors and attitudes that lay the foundation for systemic change.

Reflection for Readers

- How do adaptability, curiosity, resilience, and empowerment show up in your organization today?

- Which of these traits feels strongest in your team, and which could benefit from focused development?

Overcoming Challenges to Building a Transformation Mindset

Developing a transformation mindset is not a switch you flip—it's a shift you build. While curiosity, adaptability, resilience, and empowerment form the foundation, these traits often meet resistance from entrenched organizational habits, cognitive biases, and cultural inertia.

This section outlines five common barriers leaders must anticipate and address when cultivating transformation at scale—and how to navigate through them using practical strategies.

Risk Aversion: The Fear of Disruption

The Barrier: Organizations—especially those with legacy systems or consistent profitability—often fear experimentation. Innovation is perceived as a threat to stability, and failure is stigmatized.

Example: A global insurance firm resisted digitizing its claims process for years, despite customer frustration, because legacy teams felt more comfortable with paper-based workflows they had used for decades.

Strategy to Navigate:

Build "psychological permission" by redefining failure as feedback. Celebrate experiments, not just outcomes. Introduce structured experimentation rituals (e.g., Innovation Hours, fail-forward retrospectives) to normalize iteration and learning.

Cultural Inertia: The Weight of 'How We've Always Done It'

The Barrier: Deep-rooted processes and beliefs form invisible guardrails. Even when individuals are inspired to act differently, legacy systems often pull them back into old rhythms.

Example: In a global professional services firm, senior managers who had mastered a proven delivery model resisted adopting new digital tools. They were experts in the current way of working and feared losing credibility by experimenting with newer, unfamiliar methods. Even though younger team members were eager to innovate, the organization's performance plateaued because transformation felt like a threat to those who had built their identity around existing competencies.

Strategy to Navigate:

Surface and question the unwritten norms that keep people anchored to the past. Use real stories of success from within the organization to challenge the belief that "this is how we've always done it." Then, reinforce the shift by aligning systems—such as performance reviews, communication routines, and meeting agendas—with the new behaviors you want to promote.

Cognitive Overload: Too Much Change, Too Fast

The Barrier: When transformation efforts lack coherence or clarity, they overwhelm rather than inspire. Leaders may introduce too many initiatives, diluting focus and exhausting teams.

Example: At a high-growth e-commerce startup, the leadership team pushed for rapid product launches to stay ahead of the competition. While this velocity created initial momentum, it soon led to constant firefighting, short-term wins, and employee burnout. Long-term strategic initiatives—like improving the customer experience and strengthening platform stability—were sidelined repeatedly. Everyone was busy, but few were aligned or focused.

Strategy to Navigate:

Anchor all initiatives to a central transformation narrative. Use visual roadmaps and simplified priorities to reduce cognitive friction. Focus on *depth before breadth*—go deep with fewer changes rather than surface-level with many.

Leadership Misalignment: Mixed Signals from the Top

The Barrier: Even the most well-designed transformation stalls if senior leaders say one thing but act another. Misalignment breeds skepticism and disengagement.

Example: A financial services company proudly promoted its employee town halls and "open-door" policy as evidence of inclusion. But when a cross-functional team suggested reworking legacy compliance processes, their input was politely acknowledged but not acted upon. Over time, employees stopped voicing bold ideas, sensing that while feedback was welcomed in theory, decision-making remained top-down. Leaders were not modeling the openness they were preaching.

Strategy to Navigate:

Create visible role modeling systems. Leaders must embody the new behaviors—seek feedback publicly, host learning circles, tell vulnerability stories. Add transformation behaviors into leadership scorecards and reviews.

Lack of Reinforcement: Great Start, No Staying Power

The Barrier: Early excitement often fades without reinforcement. Without ongoing cues, recognition, and system-level alignment, new behaviors revert to old defaults.

Example: During a global digital transformation initiative, the operations team at a manufacturing company struggled to adopt data-driven decision-making. Their identity had long been tied to gut instinct, shop-floor experience, and hands-on problem solving. While training and tools were available, there were no mechanisms to reinforce or normalize the new behavior. Over time, the old ways reasserted themselves—and the transformation stalled.

Strategy to Navigate:

Reinforce consistently through structured rituals (e.g., reflection huddles, storytelling town halls), behavior-based recognition systems, and dashboards that track mindset-based KPIs like collaboration, experimentation, or learning engagement.

Key Lessons for Overcoming Challenges

1. **Empathy is Essential**: Address the emotional and psychological barriers to change with compassion. People don't resist change— they resist uncertainty and loss. Meet them where they are.

2. **Model What Matters:** Leaders must consistently demonstrate the transformation behaviors they expect from others. Culture follows the visible actions of leadership.

3. **Communicate with Purpose**: Transparent, two-way communication builds trust. Share the "why" behind the change, involve people in the process, and keep the dialogue ongoing— not just during town halls.

4. **Celebrate Progress, Not Just Outcomes**: Acknowledge small wins to sustain momentum. Recognizing effort and experimentation encourages a culture of learning and resilience.

Reflection for Readers

- Which of these barriers feels most relevant to your team or organization right now?

- What is one step you could take today to begin addressing resistance, fear, or a gap in awareness within your context?

Conclusion: The Transformative Power of Mindset

The transformation mindset is not a fixed quality—it's a learned and practiced approach to thinking, acting, and leading through change. It evolves with intention, and when nurtured, becomes the foundation for sustainable impact. In today's complex and fast-moving world, transformation isn't optional—it's essential.

The traits of adaptability, curiosity, resilience, and empowerment are not just desirable—they are indispensable for navigating disruption and unlocking human potential. Organizations that develop these traits create cultures of growth, where challenges are reframed as opportunities and setbacks become stepping stones. These organizations thrive not despite change, but because of it.

The Role of Leadership in Sustaining the Transformation Mindset

Leaders are the linchpins of transformation. Their behaviors set the tone for the entire organization. By consistently modeling the transformation mindset, fostering psychological safety, and reinforcing positive behaviors through recognition and storytelling, leaders create a ripple effect—making change feel not only possible, but energizing.

Take, for instance, a mid-sized software company that faced declining morale after multiple product failures. Instead of defaulting to blame or withdrawal, its leadership chose to reframe setbacks as growth opportunities. They introduced weekly "What We Learned" sessions and celebrated resilience and creative thinking—even when results fell short. Within a year, employee engagement surged, and the company regained its competitive edge.

This example reflects a powerful truth: transformation doesn't begin with strategy—it begins with mindset. And leaders, by showing up with intention and vulnerability, can turn that mindset into movement.

Looking Ahead

Developing a transformation mindset starts with individuals—but to unlock enterprise-level impact, it must be channeled through systems, structures, and shared language. Traits like adaptability and resilience spark change, but lasting transformation requires a framework that connects these traits to strategy, behaviors, and cultural norms at scale.

In the next part of this book, we introduce the **Catalyst Framework**—a practical, neuroscience-informed model for embedding the transformation mindset across teams and organizations. From diagnosing resistance to designing change that sticks, the Catalyst Framework provides the structure to turn mindset into movement.

Chapter Summary

- Transformation is not just a strategy—it's a **mindset**. It reflects how individuals and organizations **think, act, and respond** in the face of uncertainty and change.

- A **transformation mindset** is made up of four core traits:

  - → **Adaptability**: The ability to pivot and embrace change with confidence.

  - → **Curiosity**: A drive to explore, ask questions, and challenge assumptions.

  - → **Resilience**: The strength to bounce back from setbacks and persist through adversity.

  - → **Empowerment**: Giving people the autonomy, tools, and confidence to lead change at every level.

- These traits are not fixed—they can be **cultivated and reinforced**, creating cultures where learning, experimentation, and ownership are the norm.

- Stories and examples throughout the chapter illustrate how organizations can shift from fear, rigidity, and fixed mindsets to **growth, innovation, and agility**.

- Mindset is the **foundation for sustainable transformation**. Without it, tools and strategies will falter. With it, organizations gain the energy and resilience to evolve continuously.

- Leaders play a vital role in shaping this mindset—through modeling behaviors, building psychological safety, and recognizing progress over perfection.

Action Exercises

These exercises are designed to help you assess and develop the traits of a transformation mindset in yourself, your team, and your organization. Use them as a starting point to build momentum for growth.

1. Self-Assessment: Embracing the Four Traits

- Reflect on how well you embody adaptability, curiosity, resilience, and empowerment.

- **Action Step**:

    1. Rate yourself on a scale of 1 to 10 for each trait.

    2. Identify one trait to focus on improving over the next month.

    3. Set specific actions to develop that trait, such as seeking feedback (resilience) or experimenting with new approaches (curiosity).

2. Team Discovery: Identifying Strengths and Gaps

- Facilitate a team discussion to explore how the four traits manifest in your group's dynamics.

- **Action Step**:

    1. Ask team members to share examples of when they've demonstrated adaptability, curiosity, resilience, or empowerment.

    2. Discuss gaps and areas for growth.

    3. Collaboratively set one team goal, such as piloting a cross-functional project (curiosity) or creating a "Lessons Learned" repository (resilience).

3. Practice Curiosity: Changing the Conversation

- Curiosity starts with asking better questions. Commit to fostering curiosity in your next meeting.

- **Action Step**:

  1. Ask five open-ended questions during the meeting, such as:

     - "What would happen if we tried a completely different approach?"

     - "What's the best idea we haven't explored yet?"

  2. Observe how these questions change the tone and outcomes of the discussion.

4. Reframe a Failure: Building Resilience

- Choose a recent setback or challenge your team experienced. Use it as an opportunity to build resilience.

- **Action Step**:

  1. Hold a reflection session to discuss what went wrong, what was learned, and how it can be applied to future projects.

  2. Document these lessons and share them across the team or organization to reinforce a culture of learning.

5. Empower Others: Delegating with Purpose

- Identify one decision or responsibility you can delegate to a team member to foster empowerment.

- **Action Step**:

  1. Clearly define the task, expectations, and desired outcomes.

  2. Provide the tools and support needed for success.

  3. Acknowledge the individual's contribution publicly to reinforce their confidence and ownership.

Part II:

From Insight to Impact — Putting the Transformation Mindset into Practice

Chapter 6:

Introducing the Catalyst Framework

Transformation is not a single leap; it's a series of intentional steps. Imagine standing at the base of a mountain, gazing up at the summit. The path to the top is not always visible—it winds through dense forests, rocky terrains, and steep inclines. The climb requires preparation, determination, and the right tools to navigate unexpected challenges. The Catalyst Framework serves as your roadmap, guiding you through the complexities of transformation.

In Part 1 of this book, we explored the foundation of the transformation mindset. We learned how adaptability, resilience, and empowerment can reshape both individuals and organizations. We also uncovered how limiting beliefs and entrenched behaviors create barriers to change, while the principles of neuroplasticity offer a roadmap for rewiring these patterns.

Now, in Part 2, we shift focus from understanding transformation to **applying it**. The Catalyst Framework is the bridge between insight and action. It provides a structured yet flexible approach for navigating complex challenges, overcoming resistance, and embedding lasting change into the fabric of your organization.

This chapter introduces the Catalyst Framework—a five-phase process designed to turn strategy into action and embed transformation into daily practices. By grounding its principles in neuroplasticity, behavioural science, and leadership practice, the framework equips leaders with the tools to drive meaningful, sustainable change.

Reflection for Readers

- What transformation challenges are you currently navigating in your organization?

- How might a structured approach, like the Catalyst Framework, help you address these challenges effectively?

Recapping the Foundations of Transformation Mindset

Transformation is not a one-time destination; it is a mindset and a continuous journey. In Part 1 of this book, we laid the groundwork by exploring the essential elements of the transformation mindset. These principles now form the bedrock for the Catalyst Framework, equipping you to turn understanding into actionable strategies.

Key Insights from Part 1

1. **Neuroplasticity: Change is Possible**

   The ability of the brain to adapt and form new neural pathways underscores the potential for transformation at both individual and organizational levels. Through repetition, reinforcement, and new experiences, entrenched patterns can be rewired to align with desired outcomes.

2. **Limiting Beliefs: Invisible Barriers to Progress**

   These deeply held assumptions act as psychological roadblocks, reinforcing the status quo and stifling innovation. Identifying and challenging these beliefs is critical to unlocking both individual and organizational potential.

3. **The Traits of a Transformation Mindset: Adaptability, Curiosity, Resilience, and Empowerment**

   A transformation mindset is defined by behaviors and attitudes that thrive in complexity. These traits foster creativity, collaboration, and sustained momentum in the face of challenges.

4. **Rewiring Individuals and Organizations**

   Transformation extends beyond individuals to encompass organizational systems, structures, and cultural norms. By dismantling outdated processes and fostering collaborative environments, organizations can adapt to an ever-changing landscape.

From Mindset to Methodology

The Catalyst Framework synthesizes these foundational principles into a practical, action-oriented methodology. By integrating insights from Part 1, the framework provides a roadmap to identify challenges, create solutions, and sustain progress. It transforms understanding into action, enabling organizations to navigate complexity with clarity and confidence.

Reflection for Readers

- Which lessons from Part 1 resonate most with the challenges you or your organization are currently facing?

- How can these foundational insights help you address barriers and seize opportunities?

The Story Behind the Catalyst Framework

The Catalyst Framework was not born in a single moment of inspiration—it emerged from years of practical experience, research, and iterative refinement. Working with leaders across industries, I saw a recurring challenge: transformation efforts often failed not due to a lack of strategy or resources but because organizations struggled to bridge the gap between intention and execution.

The Gaps I Observed

Through my work in transformation, I noticed several consistent pain points in organizations attempting change:

1. **The Knowing-Doing Gap** – Leaders understood the need for change but couldn't translate knowledge into sustained action.

2. **Resistance to Change** – Employees clung to old ways, even when new approaches were clearly beneficial.

3. **Fragmented Efforts** – Initiatives lacked a cohesive structure, leading to confusion, inefficiency, and disengagement.

4. **Failure to Sustain Change** – Organizations treated transformation as a one-time project rather than a continuous journey.

Each of these challenges pointed to a missing piece in existing transformation models—a framework that didn't just guide organizations on what to change but provided a structured yet flexible roadmap on how to execute, embed, and sustain that change.

Blending Science, Experience, and Practicality

To create a solution that worked in real-world corporate environments, I drew from three key domains:

1. **Behavioral Science & Neuroscience** – Understanding how people adopt and sustain change at the neurological and psychological level.

2. **Business & Organizational Strategy** – Studying transformation methodologies used by Fortune 500 companies and refining best practices.

3. **Real-World Applications** – Testing different change models in various industries, identifying what worked consistently across teams, cultures, and structures.

I synthesized these insights into five distinct yet interdependent phases that serve as the foundation of the Catalyst Framework.

The Iterative Refinement Process

This framework wasn't perfect from the start—it evolved through trial, failure, and refinement over several years:

- Initial Version: A simplified three-step model focused only on execution, which worked but failed to address early resistance and sustainability.

- Expanded to Five Phases: To account for preparatory phases (analysing and reframing) and post-execution reinforcement (sustaining).

- Tested Across Multiple Industries: From telecom, banking, manufacturing, CPG to legacy corporations, refining the approach to ensure flexibility and repeatability.

- Final Refinements: After successfully implementing the framework in various transformation projects, I standardized it into a structured yet adaptable five-phase roadmap.

Why the Name "Catalyst"?

A catalyst in science accelerates a reaction without being consumed—just like great leaders and organizations accelerate transformation without burning out. The framework is designed to amplify the momentum of change, providing the necessary structure while ensuring adaptability.

From Theory to Action

The Catalyst Framework is more than a methodology—it is a proven, adaptable guide for leaders to bridge the gap between strategy and execution. It ensures that transformation is not just conceptualized but operationalized, and more importantly, sustained over time.

Now, let's break down the five key phases that make up the Catalyst Framework and explore how to apply them in your transformation journey.

The Five Phases of the Catalyst Framework

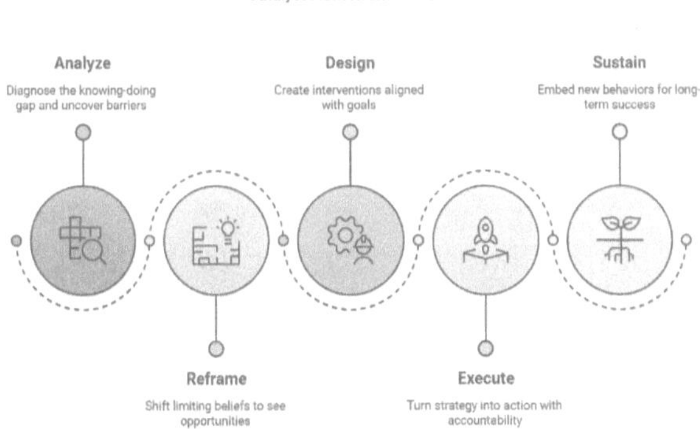

1. **Analyze**: Diagnose the knowing-doing gap, uncover barriers to transformation, and surface root causes of resistance which lead to knowing-doing gap.

2. **Reframe**: Shift limiting beliefs and narratives, enabling individuals and teams to see opportunities where they once saw obstacles.

3. **Design**: Create behavioral interventions, systems, and structures aligned with the desired mindset and organizational goals.

4. **Execute**: Turn strategy into action, ensuring accountability, momentum, and adaptability through feedback loops.

5. **Sustain**: Embed new behaviors, systems, and cultural norms into the organization's DNA to ensure long-term success.

The Science Behind the Catalyst Framework

The Catalyst Framework is not just a theoretical model—it is built upon proven scientific principles that enable sustainable transformation. By integrating insights from neuroplasticity, behavioral science, and leadership practice, it provides a structured and actionable roadmap for understanding, implementing, and sustaining transformation.

These foundational principles are explored in Part 1 and Part 2 of this book. While Part 1 delves into neuroplasticity and its role in rewiring mindsets, Part 2 further explores how behavioral science and leadership practice drive transformation at an organizational level.

This section focuses specifically on how the Catalyst Framework applies these scientific principles to accelerate change and embed lasting transformation.

Neuroplasticity: Rewiring for Change in Transformation Initiatives

As discussed in Part 1, neuroplasticity—the brain's ability to rewire itself through repetition, reinforcement, and environmental cues—is a critical driver of transformation. Just as the brain can strengthen or weaken neural pathways, organizations must intentionally build and reinforce new ways of working.

The Catalyst Framework applies neuroplasticity in two key ways:

1. Identifying and Weakening Unproductive Pathways

   ○ Just as the brain prunes unused neural connections, organizations must phase out outdated processes, rigid hierarchies, and behaviors that hinder transformation.

- ○ Example: A global retail company moved from time-consuming approval hierarchies to a decentralized decision-making model, eliminating bottlenecks and reinforcing agility and autonomy.

2. Strengthening New, Productive Pathways

- ○ Through repetition and reinforcement, organizations can embed new behaviors and cultural norms until they become second nature.

- ○ Example: A financial institution transitioning to customer-centricity introduced weekly storytelling sessions where employees shared success stories. Over time, this ingrained a culture of relationship-driven service.

For a deeper dive into neuroplasticity, refer back to Part 1, where we explored its mechanics and implications for transformation.

Behavioural Science: Bridging Knowing and Doing

One of the most significant challenges in transformation is the Knowing-Doing Gap—the disconnect between understanding what needs to change and actually implementing that change. Behavioral science helps us bridge this gap by ensuring that transformation is not just conceptualized but executed and reinforced effectively.

The Catalyst Framework applies behavioral science principles across its phases, particularly in how change is designed, executed, and sustained. It ensures that new behaviors are not only adopted but also reinforced through structured interventions and reinforcement mechanisms. To achieve this, it leverages BJ Fogg's Behavior Model, which identifies three essential elements that drive behavior change.

1. Motivation: Aligning Change with Personal and Organizational Goals

- ○ Change is more likely to succeed when people see its relevance to their personal or professional growth.

- ○ Example: A retail chain transitioning to digital-first operations framed the shift as an opportunity for employees to develop new skills, increasing engagement and reducing resistance.

2. Ability: Making Action Feasible and Effortless

    ○ When new behaviors are too complex, even motivated individuals struggle to act. The framework ensures that transformation is simplified, accessible, and practical.

    ○ Example: A healthcare organization improved hand hygiene compliance by strategically placing sanitizer stations and using visual reminders, making the action effortless.

3. Prompts: Reinforcing Change with Strategic Triggers

    ○ Timely nudges and structured cues help ensure that desired behaviors become habitual.

    ○ Example: A project management tool introduced automated reminders prompting teams to update progress regularly, improving accountability and collaboration.

These principles will be explored in detail in Chapter 9: Design – Building Behavioral Change, where we dive into habit formation, reinforcement mechanisms, and practical applications of behavioral science in organizational transformation.

Leadership Practice: Modelling and Sustaining Change

Transformation is not just about systems and processes—it requires leaders to actively model, reinforce, and sustain the behaviors that drive change. Without leadership alignment, even the most well-designed transformation efforts can falter.

The Catalyst Framework embeds leadership practice into every phase to ensure transformation is not just mandated but demonstrated.

1. Modeling Change Through Leadership Actions

    ○ Leaders set the tone for transformation by demonstrating adaptability, resilience, and curiosity.

    ○ Example: During a cultural transformation, a CEO actively participated in employee training programs, reinforcing that continuous learning applied to everyone, including leadership.

2. Reinforcing New Behaviors with Recognition & Rewards

   - For change to stick, it must be consistently reinforced. Leaders must recognize and reward behaviors that align with transformation goals.

   - Example: A manufacturing company transitioning to agile practices publicly celebrated managers who successfully implemented the new methodologies, motivating others to follow suit.

3. Embedding Change into Organizational Culture

   - Leadership commitment prevents organizations from regressing into old habits.

   - Example: A bank transitioning to a digital-first strategy introduced monthly leadership town halls to maintain focus and alignment on transformation goals.

◈ These leadership strategies will be covered in-depth in Chapters 11 and 12, where we discuss execution, accountability, leadership modeling, and sustaining cultural transformation.

Reflection for Readers

- How might the principles of neuroplasticity, behavioral science, and leadership practice shape your approach to transformation?

- Which of these principles could you leverage to address current challenges in your organization?

Chapter Summary

Transformation isn't a one-time event—it's a **structured journey**. The **Catalyst Framework** provides a practical roadmap to navigate this journey by translating mindset into sustained action.

- Built on years of real-world application, behavioral science, and neuroscience, the framework addresses critical transformation gaps:

- → The **Knowing-Doing Gap**

- → **Resistance to change**

- → **Fragmented initiatives**

- → The **failure to sustain progress**

- The framework consists of **five distinct phases**:

  - **Analyze** – Diagnose barriers and resistance.

  - **Reframe** – Shift limiting beliefs and mental models.

  - **Design** – Develop behaviors, systems, and structures aligned to transformation.

  - **Execute** – Activate strategies with feedback, accountability, and iteration.

  - **Sustain** – Embed new habits, rituals, and culture into the organization's DNA.

- **Neuroplasticity** underpins the framework by showing how organizations can "rewire" themselves through **repetition**, **reinforcement**, and **environmental support**.

- **Behavioral science** ensures change sticks by aligning transformation with motivation, simplifying new behaviors, and reinforcing them with clear prompts.

- **Leadership practice** is embedded throughout—transformation only succeeds when leaders **model**, **reinforce**, and **normalize** the desired change.

- The Catalyst Framework is both **rigorous and flexible**, enabling organizations to move from reactive change efforts to **intentional, sustained transformation.**

Action Exercises

1. Identify Your Transformation Landscape

Objective: Reflect on the transformation challenges in your organization and assess how a structured approach like the Catalyst Framework could help.

Steps:

- Identify a significant transformation challenge in your organization (e.g., cultural change, digital transformation, process reengineering).

- Analyze how transformation efforts have been approached so far:

  - Have past efforts been successful, stalled, or abandoned?

  - What were the biggest obstacles to implementation?

  - Did the organization have a structured roadmap for change, or was it fragmented?

- Compare these observations with the structured approach of the Catalyst Framework and identify where a more systematic method could have made a difference.

Deliverable: Document key insights about how your organization has handled transformation in the past and identify gaps where a framework could help.

2. The Knowing-Doing Gap Reflection

Objective: Assess where your organization struggles with moving from strategy to action and how the Catalyst Framework can help close the Knowing-Doing Gap.

Steps:

- Reflect on a past or current transformation initiative that didn't achieve its expected outcomes.

- Identify specific factors that contributed to the Knowing-Doing Gap:

    ○ Was there clear strategic intent, but poor execution?

    ○ Did leadership support the change, but teams resist adopting it?

    ○ Were there silos, bottlenecks, or a lack of accountability?

- Consider how a structured five-phase framework could have addressed these issues and helped bridge the gap.

Deliverable: Write down two to three insights about why past transformations stalled and how applying a structured framework could have improved execution.

3. Catalyst Framework Awareness Session

Objective: Introduce the Catalyst Framework to your team and explore its potential relevance to your organization.

Steps:

- Host a short discussion or presentation explaining the Catalyst Framework's five phases.

- Encourage team members to share their own experiences with transformation challenges and where structure was lacking.

- Brainstorm how the Catalyst Framework could be integrated into upcoming transformation efforts.

Deliverable: Capture key team insights and reflections on how a structured approach could improve ongoing and future transformation initiatives.

4. Recognizing Patterns of Resistance to Change

Objective: Analyze how resistance to change has manifested in past transformation efforts and how it aligns with challenges identified in the chapter.

Steps:

- Identify one past transformation effort that faced significant resistance.

- Reflect on where the resistance stemmed from:

  ○ Individuals: Fear of uncertainty, lack of skills, skepticism about leadership commitment.

  ○ Teams: Siloed mindsets, misaligned incentives, workload concerns.

  ○ Organization-wide: Conflicting priorities, bureaucracy, unclear vision.

- Think about how a structured framework like Catalyst could help address these resistance points systematically.

Deliverable: Document three major resistance patterns your organization has faced and identify potential strategies the Catalyst Framework could offer to overcome them.

5. Defining Your Transformation Vision

Objective: Establish a clear transformation vision that aligns with the structured approach of the Catalyst Framework.

Steps:

- Define one major transformation goal for your organization or team.

- Ensure your goal is:

  ○ Clear & specific (not just "improve processes" but "reduce decision-making delays by 30%").

  ○ Aligned with strategic objectives and long-term vision.

  ○ Realistic & measurable so progress can be tracked.

- Consider how the Catalyst Framework's structured approach can support this transformation.

Deliverable: Write down a one-paragraph transformation vision statement and reflect on how the Catalyst Framework can turn it into reality.

Reflection for Readers

- What transformation challenges are you currently navigating in your organization?

- How might a structured approach like the **Catalyst Framework** help you address these challenges effectively?

- Which of these exercises can you implement today to begin applying the principles of structured transformation?

Chapter 7:

Analyze: Surfacing the Knowing-Doing Gap

Imagine standing at the edge of a chasm. On one side lies knowledge—the clear understanding of what needs to be done. On the other side is action—the consistent, intentional application of that knowledge to achieve results. The Knowing-Doing Gap is the space in between—a divide that prevents individuals and organizations from realizing their full potential.

This gap is not a product of ignorance or lack of capability. In fact, most organizations know what they need to do to succeed. They talk about collaboration, innovation, and customer-centricity, yet their actions often fail to align with these principles. The result? Stalled progress, frustration, and lost trust.

The first phase of the Catalyst Framework, **Analyze**, is designed to surface and address this gap. By diagnosing barriers to action and uncovering the hidden narratives—what we call **anti-stories**—leaders can identify the root causes of inaction and create the clarity needed to move forward. This phase is the foundation of transformation, ensuring that knowledge is not just understood but applied effectively.

In this chapter, we will:

1. Define the Knowing-Doing Gap and how it manifests in individuals and organizations.

2. Explore the common barriers to action, including limiting beliefs, misaligned incentives, and cultural inertia.

3. Introduce the concept of anti-stories and their impact on behavior and decision-making.

4. Explain how neuroplasticity principles can help rewire these gaps.

5. Provide a practical exercise, **Mapping the Knowing-Doing Gap**, to help leaders identify and address their organization's challenges.

Transformation begins with understanding. By addressing the Knowing-Doing Gap, leaders can align knowledge and action, unlocking the potential for lasting and meaningful change.

Reflection for Readers:

- Where do you see gaps between what is known and what is done in your organization?

- How might diagnosing these gaps create new opportunities for progress and alignment?

What is the Knowing-Doing Gap?

The Knowing-Doing Gap represents the disconnect between understanding what needs to be done and taking consistent action to achieve it. This gap is not caused by ignorance or lack of intent but by systemic, cultural, and psychological barriers that stall progress. Leaders may recognize the importance of collaboration, innovation, or customer focus, yet their organizations struggle to translate these priorities into action.

This gap is pervasive across industries and manifests in statements like:

- "We know collaboration is important, but silos still dominate our culture."

- "We say we value innovation, but we keep using the same outdated processes."

- "We ask for employee feedback, but we rarely act on it."

This disconnect isn't about laziness or incompetence. It often stems from fear, misaligned incentives, or an adherence to the status quo.

Why Does the Gap Persist?

Understanding why the Knowing-Doing Gap exists requires examining the factors that maintain it. These include:

1. **Comfort with Familiarity**

   People naturally gravitate toward routines and processes they know, even if they're inefficient. Familiarity provides a sense of security, making change feel risky.

2. **Fear of Failure**

   The potential costs of change—financial, reputational, or personal—can loom larger than the potential benefits. This fear creates paralysis, keeping individuals and teams stuck in place.

3. **Systemic Barriers**

   Misaligned incentives, unclear priorities, or rigid hierarchies often block action. For example, when departments are rewarded for individual performance over collaboration, teamwork falters.

4. **Cultural Inertia**

   Deeply embedded norms and unwritten rules create resistance to change. Even when leaders advocate for new approaches, employees may hesitate, fearing judgment or failure.

Real-Life Example: A Financial Services Firm's Struggle

A financial services firm positioned itself as customer-centric in its branding but had internal processes designed solely for operational efficiency. Leaders acknowledged this misalignment but feared that changing workflows might disrupt their teams. This hesitation exacerbated the Knowing-Doing Gap, leading to declining customer satisfaction and stagnating growth. Only after leadership aligned incentives with customer outcomes and simplified processes did the firm close the gap and restore customer trust.

The Ripple Effects of Inaction

When the Knowing-Doing Gap is left unaddressed, the consequences ripple across an organization:

1. **Eroded Trust**: Employees and stakeholders lose confidence when actions don't align with stated priorities.

2. **Missed Opportunities**: Fear and inertia prevent organizations from capitalizing on new ideas or trends.

3. **Stagnation**: Outdated practices reduce competitiveness and hinder innovation.

Reflection for Readers:

- Where do you see evidence of the Knowing-Doing Gap in your team or organization?

- What fears or barriers might be reinforcing these gaps?

Barriers to Action in Teams and Organizations

Understanding the Knowing-Doing Gap begins with identifying the barriers that prevent individuals and teams from taking action. These barriers are often invisible, deeply embedded in organizational systems, cultural norms, or personal psychology. Addressing them is critical to enabling meaningful change.

1. Limiting Beliefs: The Stories We Tell Ourselves

As discussed in detail in chapter 3, the Limiting beliefs are assumptions that constrain thinking and behavior. They manifest as unspoken rules like, "This is how we've always done it," or "Change is too risky." These beliefs feel like truths but are often rooted in fear or past failures.

Story: A Manufacturing Company's Resistance to Automation

A manufacturing company knew that automating their production line would increase efficiency, but leaders resisted, fearing disruptions and employee backlash. By piloting automation on a small scale and engaging employees in the process, leadership reframed their belief from "Automation will create chaos" to "Automation will empower employees with higher-value work." The success of the pilot built confidence and paved the way for broader adoption.

Reflection for Readers:

- What unspoken rules or assumptions might be holding your team back?

- How can you reframe these beliefs to focus on opportunities rather than risks?

2. Lack of Clarity: The Paralysis of Uncertainty

Ambiguity in goals or priorities often paralyzes teams. When success isn't clearly defined or priorities conflict, even motivated individuals may struggle to act.

Example: A Tech Startup's Scattered Priorities

A tech startup aimed to improve customer retention but was unsure whether to focus on product features, customer support, or loyalty programs. The lack of clarity led to scattered efforts with minimal impact. Once leadership aligned around a single goal—enhancing customer support—they concentrated resources, achieved measurable improvements, and gained momentum for future projects.

Reflection for Readers:

- Are your team's goals specific, measurable, and clearly communicated?

- How might simplifying priorities create momentum?

3. Misaligned Incentives: When Systems Work Against Goals

Incentives that reward individual or departmental performance over collective outcomes exacerbate the Knowing-Doing Gap. Teams often prioritize their own success at the expense of broader organizational goals.

Case Study: Breaking Silos in Retail

A retail chain's incentive system rewarded store managers based on individual profits, discouraging collaboration on company-wide initiatives. Leadership redesigned the system to include shared metrics, like customer satisfaction and regional sales growth. This change encouraged managers to work together, aligning efforts with the company's long-term goals.

Reflection for Readers:

- Do your incentive structures align with your organizational goals?

- How might adjusting rewards foster collaboration and alignment?

4. Cultural Inertia: The Weight of Tradition

Deeply embedded cultural norms often reinforce the status quo. Even when individuals recognize the need for change, they may fear challenging established practices.

Story: Shifting Hierarchies in Healthcare

In a healthcare organization, a culture of deference to senior leaders stifled innovation. Junior staff hesitated to propose ideas, fearing criticism. Leadership addressed this inertia by creating forums where all levels of staff could contribute and be recognized. Over time, this initiative shifted the culture, enabling open dialogue and creative problem-solving.

Reflection for Readers:

- What cultural norms in your organization reinforce the status quo?

- How can you create safe spaces for employees to challenge existing practices?

The Interplay of Barriers

These barriers often reinforce one another:

- Limiting beliefs fuel cultural inertia.

- Lack of clarity exacerbates misaligned incentives.

- Misaligned systems create environments where cultural inertia thrives.

To close the Knowing-Doing Gap, leaders must look beyond surface symptoms and address these root causes.

Reflection for Readers:

- Which of these barriers resonates most with your organization's current challenges?

- How might addressing these barriers unlock new opportunities for progress?

Anti-Stories: The Narratives That Hold Us Back

Beneath every Knowing-Doing Gap lies a set of underlying narratives that justify inaction. These are called Anti-Stories—negative assumptions or perspectives that masquerade as truths. They often feel rational, but they are deeply rooted in fear, past failures, or resistance to change.

Anti-Stories serve as barriers to develop a transformation mindset by:

- Justifying inaction – "We tried this before, and it didn't work."

- Reinforcing the status quo – "If it's not broken, why fix it?"

- Exaggerating risks – "If we automate, we'll lose the personal touch that sets us apart."

These narratives discourage progress because they create a psychological comfort zone, allowing organizations to avoid risk and maintain familiar routines.

Recognizing Anti-Stories in Your Organization

Identifying Anti-Stories is the first step in closing the Knowing-Doing Gap. Organizations often repeat limiting narratives that reinforce inaction, such as:

◈ "We lack the expertise to make this work." → Rooted in fear of failure

◈ "We don't have the resources to change." → Reflects scarcity mindset rather than innovation thinking

◈ "This is how we've always done it." → Indicates cultural inertia and resistance to experimentation

To surface these narratives, leaders should:

- Listen for repeated excuses in meetings, strategy discussions, and resistance to new initiatives.

- Ask why past efforts stalled and look for common reasoning patterns.

- Encourage teams to articulate their concerns—many Anti-Stories operate beneath the surface.

Anti-Stories Identification to Reframing

Recognizing these limiting narratives is the first step in closing the Knowing-Doing Gap.

In Chapter 9: Reframe – Shifting Anti-Stories, we will explore how to challenge and replace these narratives with empowering perspectives. Through practical exercises and real-world case studies, you will learn how to reframe Anti-Stories into narratives that promote action, innovation, and transformation.

The Role of Neuroplasticity in Bridging the Gap

In Part 1, we explored the science of neuroplasticity—the brain's ability to reorganize itself by forming new neural pathways through repetition and reinforcement. These same principles apply not just to individuals but to organizations navigating transformation.

The Knowing-Doing Gap persists because ingrained organizational habits, outdated workflows, and cultural inertia create deeply embedded pathways of inaction—just as the brain defaults to familiar patterns. Bridging this gap requires rewiring these entrenched organizational behaviors, much like how the brain forms new neural pathways when learning a skill.

Applying Neuroplasticity Principles to Organizations

The Catalyst Framework applies neuroplasticity-inspired principles to help organizations close the Knowing-Doing Gap:

1. Repetition: Strengthening New Pathways

Why it matters: Just as repeated actions strengthen neural pathways, reinforcing new ways of working helps organizations establish productive behaviors as defaults.

Example: A professional services firm that struggled with a lack of feedback culture introduced weekly check-ins to normalize open communication. Over time, structured repetition rewired their workplace culture, making feedback a natural habit.

Actionable Insight: Identify one behavior critical to bridging the Knowing-Doing Gap and create opportunities to practice it consistently.

2. Reinforcement: Embedding New Behaviors

Why it matters: The brain retains reinforced behaviors, and organizations do the same when they reward actions that align with transformation goals.

Example: A telecom company that wanted to become more customer-centric recognized and celebrated teams that improved customer satisfaction. This reinforced the importance of customer-first behavior, embedding it into the company's DNA.

Actionable Insight: Use storytelling, recognition, and rewards to reinforce desired behaviors and align them with organizational values.

3. Exposure: Challenging Entrenched Assumptions

Why it matters: Exposure to new perspectives and experiences disrupts old patterns and fosters adaptability.

Example: A healthcare system struggling with silos paired administrative and clinical teams for problem-solving workshops. This cross-functional exposure broke down barriers, leading to more collaborative care.

Actionable Insight: Create opportunities for exposure through cross-functional projects, external benchmarking, or industry partnerships.

Connecting Neuroplasticity to the Catalyst Framework

These principles of Repetition, Reinforcement, and Exposure are embedded into every phase of the Catalyst Framework:

1. Analyze – Identify entrenched habits and processes that reinforce the Knowing-Doing Gap.

2. Reframe – Replace limiting narratives with empowering perspectives that align with transformation goals.

3. Design – Build structures and interventions that encourage repetition and reinforcement of desired behaviors.

4. Execute – Apply changes consistently to establish new workplace habits.

5. Sustain – Reinforce transformation through ongoing recognition, rewards, and continued exposure to new perspectives.

By aligning transformation efforts with neuroplasticity-driven strategies, organizations can break free from inertia, turn strategy into sustained action, and successfully bridge the Knowing-Doing Gap.

Reflection for Readers

- What behaviors or mindsets in your organization need to be rewired?

- How might repetition, reinforcement, or exposure accelerate this process?

Chapter Summary

- The **Knowing-Doing Gap** is the disconnect between knowing what needs to be done and consistently acting on it. It's not a result of ignorance—but of **fear, inertia, misaligned incentives, and cultural resistance**.

- The **Analyze phase** of the Catalyst Framework helps leaders **diagnose barriers** to action, surface unspoken narratives ("anti-stories"), and identify systemic causes of inaction.

- Key organizational barriers include:

→ **Limiting beliefs** (e.g., "This is how we've always done it")

→ **Lack of clarity** around priorities and goals

→ **Misaligned incentives** that reward individual over collective outcomes

→ **Cultural inertia** rooted in fear of judgment or breaking tradition

- **Anti-stories** are limiting narratives that justify inaction and preserve the status quo. Examples include "We don't have the resources to change" or "It failed before, so it won't work now."

- Applying **neuroplasticity principles** (repetition, reinforcement, and exposure) helps organizations rewire these outdated behaviors and embed new pathways:

  - **Repetition** builds consistency in new habits

  - **Reinforcement** embeds change through recognition and rewards

  - **Exposure** challenges assumptions through cross-functional collaboration or external insights

- The Analyze phase is not just about diagnosing problems— it sets the stage for transformation by creating **awareness, clarity, and alignment** between intent and action.

Action Exercises

The following exercises will help you identify, analyze, and surface key blockers that prevent transformation from moving forward. By actively reflecting on these gaps, you can begin to uncover hidden barriers, anti-stories, and misaligned systems that hold back progress.

1. Identifying the Knowing-Doing Gap in Your Organization

Objective: Recognize specific areas where there is a disconnect between what your organization knows and what it actually does.

Steps:

- Identify one or two areas where your organization has clear knowledge of best practices but struggles with execution. Examples:

  - Leadership promotes collaboration, but silos persist.

  - Teams acknowledge the need for customer-centricity, yet internal processes prioritize efficiency over customer needs.

- Ask: What factors might be reinforcing this gap?

  - Fear of failure, lack of clarity, misaligned incentives, or cultural inertia?

- Capture specific real-world examples where the organization says one thing but does another.

Deliverable: Write a one-page gap analysis highlighting 2-3 disconnects between strategy and execution.

2. Diagnosing the Barriers to Action

Objective: Uncover the systemic, cultural, and psychological barriers that reinforce the Knowing-Doing Gap.

Steps:

- Using the four major barriers from the chapter (Limiting Beliefs, Lack of Clarity, Misaligned Incentives, Cultural Inertia), assess how each one plays a role in your organization:

  ○ Limiting Beliefs: What unspoken assumptions are preventing change?

  ○ Lack of Clarity: Are goals, priorities, and roles clearly defined?

  ○ Misaligned Incentives: Do performance metrics encourage the wrong behaviors?

  ○ Cultural Inertia: What historical norms reinforce the status quo?

- Conduct a team discussion or leadership reflection to identify real-world examples of these barriers in action.

Deliverable: Create a ranked list of top barriers with insights on their root causes.

3. Anti-Stories Discovery Session

Objective: Identify the limiting narratives (Anti-Stories) that justify inaction and reinforce the Knowing-Doing Gap.

Steps:

- Gather a small team or leadership group and ask them to list common anti-stories that reinforce stagnation. Examples:

  ○ "We've tried this before, and it didn't work."

  ○ "If it's not broken, why fix it?"

  ○ "This won't work here—we're different."

- For each anti-story, identify its root cause:

  ○ *Is it based on past failure? Fear of uncertainty? A lack of resources?*

- Record these Anti-Stories for future reference—Chapter 9 will focus on reframing them into empowering narratives.

Deliverable: Document a list of 3-5 Anti-Stories that exist in your organization.

4. Mapping the Systemic Forces Behind the Gap

Objective: Use systems thinking to uncover how different organizational elements interact to reinforce the Knowing-Doing Gap.

Steps:

- Create a cause-and-effect diagram to explore how different forces contribute to the gap. Example:

  - Leadership sets transformation goals → Middle management faces conflicting priorities → Employees feel disengaged → No action is taken → Goals remain unachieved.

- Identify which elements in this system are controllable and where small interventions might create the most leverage for change.

- Discuss with stakeholders: *If we changed one part of this system, what would happen?*

Deliverable: Develop a visual representation of how systemic factors reinforce the Knowing-Doing Gap in your organization.

5. Actionable Steps to Start Closing the Gap

Objective: Based on insights from previous exercises, define small, practical steps to begin addressing the Knowing-Doing Gap.

Steps:

- Review your gap analysis, barrier assessment, anti-story discovery, and system mapping to identify one high-impact area to address.

- Define a low-risk experiment to test closing the gap in a controlled setting. Examples:

  - Introduce a new incentive aligned with collaboration.

  - Test a new meeting format that reinforces decision-making clarity.

  - Challenge a widely accepted anti-story in an all-hands meeting.

- Assign clear accountability for the initiative and set short-term measurement criteria to track its effectiveness.

Deliverable: Write a one-page action plan for a small-scale intervention to test in your organization.

Reflection for Readers

- Which of these exercises feels most relevant to the Knowing-Doing Gap in your organization?

- How can you use these exercises to align behaviors and systems with your transformation goals?

Chapter 8

Reframe: Shifting Anti-Stories

In the previous chapter, we delved into the Knowing-Doing Gap, uncovering the barriers to action and identifying the anti-stories that hold individuals and organizations back. The Analyze phase provided the clarity needed to understand where transformation stalls. Now, in the Reframe phase of the Catalyst Framework, we take the next critical step: challenging those anti-stories and replacing them with empowering narratives.

Reframing is a powerful tool for unlocking potential. It allows organizations to transform limiting beliefs into actionable opportunities and build a foundation for sustainable change. Imagine a team paralyzed by the belief that "failure is unacceptable." Reframing that narrative to "failure is a stepping stone to success" not only shifts the mindset but also enables risk-taking, learning, and innovation. Reframing doesn't just happen in the mind—it happens in the brain. Through neuroplasticity, these new perspectives create lasting neural pathways, reinforcing behaviors that drive progress.

This chapter explores the transformative power of reframing, emphasizing how it bridges the gap between knowledge and action. By the end, you'll have practical strategies to identify anti-stories, challenge their validity, and embed empowering narratives into your team's culture.

Reflection for Readers:

- What narratives within your organization are preventing progress or innovation?

- How might shifting these narratives create new possibilities?

The Power of Reframing

Reframing is the process of shifting perspective, replacing limiting beliefs or anti-stories with empowering narratives that foster progress and innovation. It is a mental pivot that unlocks new possibilities and breaks through perceived barriers.

Imagine looking through a small window, believing it shows the full view of the world outside. Reframing is like stepping outside and realizing the landscape is far broader than you initially perceived. It reveals not just **one path forward**, but multiple opportunities waiting to be explored. In an organizational context, reframing moves teams from "We can't" to "We could," and ultimately, "We will".

Why Reframing Matters

Reframing is essential for driving transformation because it addresses the foundational beliefs that influence behavior. A team that sees obstacles instead of opportunities will naturally resist change, while a team empowered with a new perspective will act with confidence and creativity.

Key Benefits of Reframing:

1. **Uncovering Opportunities:** It enables teams to see potential where they once saw barriers.

2. **Building Confidence:** By shifting narratives, reframing reduces fear and resistance, creating a pathway for action.

3. **Fostering Innovation:** Reframing challenges entrenched assumptions, encouraging creative problem-solving.

Example: Reframing Risk in a Financial Institution

A global financial institution hesitated to adopt AI-powered automation, driven by the anti-story: *"AI is too risky and will replace human jobs."* This fear-based narrative stalled innovation, leaving the company behind as competitors embraced AI-driven efficiencies.

Reframe: Leadership shifted the focus to: *"AI enhances decision-making, eliminates routine tasks, and empowers employees for higher-value roles."*

- Instead of viewing AI as a threat, the institution repositioned it as a tool for augmentation rather than replacement.

- Leadership launched AI awareness workshops, addressing concerns and showcasing how AI could improve job satisfaction by reducing mundane tasks.

- The company invested in upskilling programs, training employees to leverage AI-driven insights rather than fear automation.

Outcome: The institution successfully integrated AI, increasing operational efficiency, customer personalization, and risk management accuracy. Employees not only retained their roles but transitioned into higher-value strategic functions, strengthening both innovation and workforce confidence.

Reframing at Scale: Shifting Organizational Cultures

Reframing is not just a tool for individual mindset shifts—it has the power to transform entire organizational cultures. When a company's deeply ingrained narratives reinforce fear-based decision-making, they stifle innovation, risk-taking, and adaptability.

Example: A Manufacturing Company's Shift from Fear to Innovation

A global manufacturing company operated under the anti-story:

"Failure is unacceptable."

This belief discouraged experimentation, leading to rigid processes, missed opportunities, and a culture of playing it safe. Employees hesitated to propose new ideas, fearing repercussions if things didn't go as planned.

The Reframe: "Failure is a stepping stone to success."

Actions Taken:

1. **Leadership Role Modeling** – Senior executives openly shared stories of past failures that led to major innovations, reinforcing that setbacks fuel growth rather than end careers.

2. **Recognition for Experimentation** – Instead of only celebrating success, teams were rewarded for bold ideas, even when results

fell short. Leaders introduced an "Innovative Failure" award, normalizing calculated risks.

3. **Embedding Storytelling into the Culture** – Team meetings and town halls highlighted resilience stories, demonstrating how learnings from past mistakes improved processes and products.

Result: Over time, this cultural shift led to:

- A pipeline of innovative product ideas, as employees felt safer experimenting.

- Higher engagement scores, with teams feeling empowered to take ownership of improvements.

- Faster problem-solving, as employees collaborated more openly without fear of blame.

Reflection for Readers:

- What limiting narratives or anti-stories are holding your team or organization back?

- How could reframing these narratives create an environment for growth and creativity?

Reframing and Neural Rewiring

Reframing is not just a cognitive shift—it is a neurological transformation. The principles of neuroplasticity reveal how repeated thought patterns strengthen neural pathways, embedding beliefs into the brain's default mode of thinking. By challenging anti-stories and replacing them with empowering narratives, individuals and organizations can rewire their mental models to align with growth and innovation.

The Science Behind Reframing

Neuroplasticity, the brain's capacity to form and reorganize neural connections, demonstrates that beliefs and behaviors are not fixed. Instead, they are shaped through repetition and reinforcement. Every time a limiting belief is replaced with an empowering narrative, the brain begins to form new pathways. With consistent reinforcement, these pathways strengthen, eventually overriding the old patterns.

Key Mechanisms of Neuroplasticity in Reframing:

1. **Repetition:** Consistent engagement with a new narrative reinforces its neural connections, making it the brain's preferred pathway.

2. **Reinforcement:** Associating new narratives with positive outcomes strengthens their impact.

3. **Exposure:** Introducing diverse perspectives and experiences challenges entrenched assumptions and accelerates rewiring.

The Role of Repetition and Reinforcement

Repetition and reinforcement are the twin engines of neural rewiring. Without consistent engagement and positive reinforcement, new narratives risk fading before they take root.

Story: Rewiring a Culture of Innovation

A global consumer goods company grappled with a risk-averse culture driven by the anti-story, "Failure is unacceptable." Leadership initiated a deliberate reframing effort to shift the narrative to, "Failure is a stepping stone to success."

Actions Taken:

1. Leaders shared examples of past failures that led to major successes.

2. Teams were encouraged to document lessons learned from setbacks and presented them during monthly "Innovation Reviews."

3. Employees who demonstrated resilience and creativity, even in failure, were celebrated in company-wide communications.

Outcome: Over time, the reframed narrative became embedded in the company's culture, resulting in a surge of innovative product launches and a 30% increase in employee satisfaction.

Practical Tips for Reinforcing New Narratives

1. **Celebrate Wins:** Recognize behaviors that align with the new narrative. For example, highlight a team's innovative approach, even if the results were imperfect.

2. **Incorporate into Rituals:** Make the reframed narrative a visible part of daily operations, such as starting meetings with lessons learned from challenges.

3. **Visual Cues:** Display reminders, such as quotes or success stories, in shared spaces to keep the new narrative top of mind.

Why Reframing Leads to Lasting Change

Reframing is powerful because it changes the way people think, not just how they act. By embedding reframed narratives into the brain's neural pathways and the organization's cultural norms, leaders can create sustainable change. Over time, these empowering narratives become the default mode of thinking and behavior, enabling individuals and teams to act with confidence and creativity.

Case Study: From "Our People Won't Embrace Data" to "We Can Learn Together"

A mid-sized manufacturing company resisted investing in analytics tools, believing, *"Our frontline teams aren't data-savvy."* This anti-story stalled progress on automation and decision-making improvements.

The Reframe: Leadership shifted the belief to, *"With the right support, our people can become confident data users."*

Actions Taken:

- Introduced simple, hands-on analytics dashboards tailored for each team's workflow.

- Piloted a "Data Buddies" program—pairing analysts with frontline supervisors to co-own small data projects.

- Used early success stories in town halls to reinforce the new mindset of collective capability.

Outcome: Within a year, over 70% of frontline teams were actively using data tools in daily decisions, contributing to a 15% improvement in production efficiency and a significant uplift in employee confidence.

Reflection for Readers:

- How might repetition and reinforcement help reframe limiting beliefs in your team or organization?

- What rituals or practices could you introduce to embed new narratives?

Practical Tool: Steps to Reframe Anti-Stories

Reframing anti-stories is a deliberate process that begins with identifying, challenging, and replacing limiting beliefs with empowering narratives. These first three steps form the foundation for mindset transformation. Once reframed narratives are in place, they can be translated into behaviors, systems, and routines—something we'll explore in the next chapter.

Step 1: Surface the Anti-Stories

The first step is to uncover the anti-stories that limit progress. These narratives often feel like unchangeable truths but are rooted in fear, past experiences, or cultural norms.

Questions to Surface Anti-Stories:

- What assumptions are we making about this challenge?

- Are these beliefs based on evidence or fear?

- How do these narratives influence our decisions and behaviors?

Example:

Anti-Story: "Our customers wouldn't pay for premium services."

Root Cause: Past failed attempts and fear of alienating the customer base.

Impact: This belief prevented the team from exploring opportunities for differentiation and revenue growth.

Step 2: Challenge the Anti-Stories

Once identified, the next step is to critically evaluate the validity of these narratives. This involves gathering evidence, analyzing assumptions, and exposing logical inconsistencies.

Questions to Challenge Anti-Stories:

- What evidence supports or contradicts this belief?
- Are there examples where this belief has been proven false?
- What might happen if we're wrong about this assumption?

Example:

A logistics company challenged the anti-story, "Automation will eliminate jobs," by analyzing data from industry peers. They discovered that companies adopting automation had actually increased employment in higher-value roles.

Step 3: Reframe the Narrative

Reframing involves shifting the limiting belief into an empowering and actionable narrative. The reframed story should inspire confidence and align with organizational goals.

Tips for Reframing:

- Use positive and possibility-focused language.
- Align the new narrative with organizational values and objectives.
- Make the narrative specific and actionable.

Example:

Anti-Story: "We don't have the resources to innovate."

Reframed Narrative: "By reallocating existing resources creatively, we can innovate

From Reframing to Reinforcement

Once anti-stories have been reframed, the next challenge is ensuring these new narratives are reinforced consistently, embedded into daily behaviors, and supported through systems, incentives, and rituals. This is where behavioral design, repetition, and reinforcement come into play.

In **Chapter 9: Design – Building Behavioral Change**, we will explore how to translate reframed narratives into sustained action, using practical tools from behavioral science and neuroplasticity to drive long-term cultural transformation.

Reflection for Readers:

- What anti-stories in your organization could benefit from this structured reframing process?

- How could you involve your team in surfacing and challenging these narratives collaboratively?

- What new narratives might inspire greater possibility, alignment, or momentum?

Real-Life Stories of Reframing

Reframing anti-stories is a transformative practice that enables individuals and organizations to challenge limiting beliefs, discover new opportunities, and drive meaningful change. Below are real-life examples that illustrate how organizations successfully reframed their narratives to unlock progress and innovation.

1. From "We're Too Small to Compete" to "Our Agility is Our Strength"

Challenge: A boutique consulting firm believed it couldn't compete with larger firms. This anti-story limited their ambition, causing them to avoid high-profile projects and miss growth opportunities.

Reframe: Leadership shifted the narrative to: "Our agility and personalized service make us uniquely valuable." They emphasized their ability to adapt quickly, tailor solutions, and build close client relationships.

Actions Taken:

- Highlighted success stories showcasing superior outcomes for clients.

- Trained the sales team to position agility as a competitive advantage.

- Piloted a high-profile project to demonstrate capabilities.

Outcome: The firm secured larger contracts, built a reputation as an innovator, and increased its client base by 35% in two years.

2. From "This Will Never Work Here" to "Let's Tailor It to Work for Us"

Challenge: A hospital resisted adopting a patient care model developed by a peer organization, claiming, "This will never work here; we're too unique." This narrative stifled progress and innovation.

Reframe: Leadership engaged staff in pilot programs, reframing the narrative to: "This could work here if we adapt it to our strengths."

Actions Taken:

- Conducted workshops to identify elements of the model that aligned with existing practices.

- Shared success stories from other hospitals to build confidence.

- Regularly updated staff on progress, fostering a sense of ownership.

Outcome: The hospital reduced wait times by 20%, improved patient outcomes, and increased staff engagement by creating a culture of innovation and collaboration.

3. From "Failure is Unacceptable" to "Failure Fuels Success"

Challenge: A manufacturing company adhered to a risk-averse culture driven by the belief, "Failure is unacceptable." This anti-story created a fear of experimentation, stifling creativity and innovation.

Reframe: Leadership shifted the narrative to: "Failure is a stepping stone to success," emphasizing the value of learning from mistakes.

Actions Taken:

- Introduced "Failure Forums" where teams shared lessons from unsuccessful projects.

- Embedded resilience training into leadership programs.

- Celebrated teams that demonstrated creativity, even when results fell short.

Outcome: The organization saw a 40% increase in R&D output over three years, with a steady pipeline of innovative products. Employee engagement also rose by 25%.

4. From "We Can't Afford Change" to "Change is an Investment in Our Future"

Challenge: A nonprofit resisted adopting digital tools, citing the belief, "We can't afford change." This anti-story masked deeper fears of disrupting workflows and alienating long-tenured staff.

Reframe: The narrative was reframed to: "Change is an investment in our future, enabling us to serve more people effectively."

Actions Taken:

- Identified cost-effective digital solutions aligned with the nonprofit's mission.

- Provided staff training to build confidence in using new tools.

- Highlighted small wins, such as improved donor engagement through automation.

Outcome: The nonprofit modernized its operations, expanded its donor base by 20%, and improved efficiency while maintaining strong relationships with existing supporters.

5. From "Our Industry is Too Traditional" to "We Can Lead Change in Our Industry"

Challenge: An agricultural company believed its industry was too traditional for technology adoption, reinforcing the anti-story, "Our industry isn't ready for change."

Reframe: Leadership shifted the narrative to: "We can lead change in our industry by showing how technology improves efficiency and sustainability."

Actions Taken:

- Partnered with a tech startup to pilot precision farming solutions.

- Shared results with key stakeholders, including farmers and industry associations.

- Positioned themselves as thought leaders by hosting conferences on agricultural innovation.

Outcome: The company gained a competitive edge, improving crop yields by 15% and attracting partnerships with global investors.

Key Lessons from These Stories

- **Start with Mindset**: Begin by shifting how challenges are framed before redesigning systems or behaviors.

- **Communicate Early Wins**: Small successes help build confidence in the new narrative.

- **Co-Create the Reframe**: Involving employees and stakeholders makes the new story more believable and actionable.

- **Track Shifts in Thinking**: Monitor how language, decision-making, and team discussions evolve in response to the reframe.

Reflection for Readers:

- Which of these stories resonates most with the challenges your organization faces?

- How might reframing your organization's anti-stories create similar opportunities for growth and transformation?

The Role of Storytelling in Reframing

1. Illustrating the Need for Change

Use storytelling to highlight the limitations of the current anti-story and the opportunities offered by the reframed narrative.

Example:

A manufacturing company shared the story of how a competitor automated its production line, achieving faster output and higher quality. This story reframed the narrative from "Automation will cost jobs" to "Automation creates higher-value opportunities for our workforce."

2. Celebrating Early Wins

Highlight stories of individuals or teams who have embraced the reframed narrative and achieved success.

Example:

A retail chain shifting to digital-first practices shared a story about a manager who used digital tools to double online sales. This reinforced the new narrative that "Digital adoption drives growth and customer satisfaction."

3. Using Customer Testimonials

Customer stories are a powerful way to show the impact of reframed narratives on end-users.

Example:

A healthcare organization transitioning to patient-centric care shared a testimonial from a patient whose experience improved due to streamlined services. This story helped teams connect emotionally to the value of the transformation.

4. Normalizing Failure Through Personal Stories

Leaders can share their own experiences of learning from failure to normalize risk-taking and challenge the anti-story, "Failure is unacceptable."

Example:

A CEO shared how an early business failure taught them resilience and inspired the creation of a successful company. This story reframed failure as a critical step in the innovation journey.

Case Study: The Power of Customer Stories in Reframing

Scenario:

A financial institution resisted adopting a customer-centric approach, driven by the anti-story, "We already know what our customers need." This mindset limited innovation and created friction between departments.

Action Taken:

Leadership collected real customer stories that highlighted gaps in the current approach. For instance:

- A customer shared how cumbersome processes discouraged them from applying for a loan.

- Another described how a competitor's seamless digital experience won their business.

Impact:

Sharing these stories during team meetings reframed the narrative to, "Listening to customers helps us innovate and retain their loyalty." Departments collaborated to redesign workflows, leading to improved customer satisfaction scores and a 20% increase in loan applications.

Tips for Using Storytelling in Reframing

1. **Be Authentic:** Use real examples and personal experiences to make stories relatable and impactful.

2. **Create Emotional Engagement:** Highlight the human element, such as customer outcomes or team achievements, to evoke empathy and connection.

3. **Align Stories with Goals:** Choose stories that reinforce the reframed narrative and align with strategic objectives.

4. **Repeat and Reinforce:** Share stories consistently across multiple channels—team meetings, newsletters, and social media—to ensure they resonate widely.

While storytelling also plays a role in reinforcing new behaviors over time, its most immediate value is in helping teams let go of old narratives and emotionally connect with a reframed perspective. It sets the stage for deeper engagement and sustained action.

Reflection for Readers:

- What stories from your organization could illustrate the benefits of reframing?

- How might storytelling help your team connect emotionally to a new narrative?

Conclusion: Reframing as a Catalyst for Transformation

Reframing is the bridge between understanding and action. It enables individuals and organizations to challenge entrenched narratives, replace them with empowering perspectives, and unlock new opportunities for growth and innovation. More than a mental shift, reframing is a foundational step in the transformation journey—it creates the mindset that drives behaviors, fosters collaboration, and sustains progress.

Reframing initiates possibility. It shifts teams from limitation to agency, from doubt to confidence. It lays the groundwork for transformation by opening space for fresh thinking and aligned belief systems. When leaders and teams begin to see challenges through new lenses, action becomes not only possible—but inevitable.

As we transition to the next phase of the Catalyst Framework, **Design**, we will explore how to translate these reframed narratives into practical systems, processes, and behaviors. Reframing sets the stage for transformation; the systems and structures we build around these narratives will make that transformation enduring.

Chapter Summary

- The **Reframe phase** addresses the anti-stories—limiting narratives that justify inaction and reinforce the Knowing-Doing Gap.

  Reframing replaces these with empowering stories that spark momentum and unlock transformation.

- Reframing **is both a mindset and a neurological process**, leveraging neuroplasticity. Repeated exposure to new narratives rewires default thinking patterns at both the individual and organizational level.

- Key reframing mechanisms include:

  → **Repetition** of the new narrative to embed it

  → **Reinforcement** through recognition, storytelling, and leadership modeling

  → **Exposure** to new perspectives that challenge old beliefs

- Real-world examples—from consulting firms to nonprofits—illustrate how reframing narratives like "We're too small to compete" or "Failure is unacceptable" led to measurable improvements in innovation, confidence, and business outcomes.

- A structured reframing process includes:

  1. **Surfacing anti-stories** (e.g., "This will never work here")

  2. **Challenging their validity** using data and perspective shifts

  3. **Replacing them with empowering narratives** aligned with strategy and values

- Storytelling **is a critical tool** in reframing—it builds emotional resonance, normalizes new thinking, and makes reframed narratives relatable and repeatable across teams.

- Reframing is not just about new language—it's about creating the mental space for bold action and systemic change.

It prepares organizations to move from intention to implementation.

Action Exercises

These exercises are designed to help leaders and teams identify, challenge, and reframe anti-stories in their organizations. Use them to shift from limiting beliefs to empowering narratives that open space for action and innovation.

1. Identify and Reframe an Anti-Story

Objective: Practice the core three-step reframing process on a limiting belief.

Action Steps:

- Write down one anti-story in your team or organization that limits progress.

- Identify its root cause (e.g., fear, past failures, unclear strategy).

- Challenge the anti-story using data, examples, or logical reasoning.

- Collaboratively reframe it with your team into a positive, actionable narrative.

Example:

- Anti-Story: "We don't have the resources to innovate."

- Reframed Narrative: "By reallocating what we already have, we can innovate without exceeding our budget."

2. Storytelling as a Reframing Tool

Objective: Use storytelling to help teams emotionally connect with a reframed narrative.

Action Steps:

- Identify a recent success story that illustrates a shift in mindset or behavior.

- Share this story in a team meeting, newsletter, or leadership update.

- Invite team members to contribute their own stories aligned with the new narrative.

3. Create a Reframing Ritual

Objective: Build reflection into regular team conversations to normalize reframing.

Action Steps:

- Dedicate time in weekly meetings for team members to share:

  - A limiting belief they encountered.

  - How they challenged or reframed it.

- Capture these reframed narratives in a shared space (whiteboard, digital tracker, etc.) to review over time.

4. Reframe with Evidence

Objective: Use real-world data and examples to challenge anti-stories.

Action Steps:

- Choose an anti-story (e.g., "Our customers won't pay for premium services").

- Gather relevant data—customer feedback, competitor benchmarks, or market trends.

- Use the insights to question the assumption and guide a new, more empowering narrative.

Reflection for Readers:

- What anti-stories in your organization are ready to be reframed?

- How can small rituals or storytelling spark collective mindset shifts?

- What new narrative would your team benefit from believing right now?

Chapter 9:

Design: Building Behavioural Change

Transformation is only as strong as the behaviors that sustain it. Imagine an architect designing a bridge to connect two distant points. Without a solid structure, the bridge will collapse under its own weight, rendering it useless no matter how visionary the blueprint. Similarly, transformation efforts, no matter how well-planned, will fail without carefully designed behaviors to support and sustain them.

In the Catalyst Framework, the Design phase builds on the reframed narratives established in the previous phase. These narratives—such as "Failure fuels growth" or "Customers are partners"—are critical to transformation. But without tangible, repeatable behaviors to reinforce them, these narratives remain theoretical. The Design phase translates reframed beliefs into systems, cues, and actions that embed transformation into daily routines and culture.

Behavioral change is not automatic. Even the most motivated teams can revert to old habits if the systems around them are misaligned or if behaviors feel too complex to sustain. This is where deliberate behavioral design becomes essential. Leveraging insights from behavioral science and neuroplasticity, this phase ensures that transformation moves from intent to impact.

In this chapter, we will:

- Explore **Fogg's Behavior Model (FBM)** as a roadmap for designing and sustaining behavior.

- Connect behavioral interventions to the reframed narratives established in the Reframe phase.

- Use real-world, Fortune 50-level examples to illustrate behavioral design at scale.

- Provide a practical framework for designing, testing, and reinforcing behavioral change.

By the end of this chapter, you'll have the tools to design systems and cues that drive lasting transformation, embedding reframed narratives into your organization's culture.

Fogg's Behavior Model: A Roadmap for Action

Behavioral change doesn't happen randomly—it occurs when the right conditions are in place. Developed by Dr. BJ Fogg, the Fogg Behavior Model (FBM) provides a practical framework for understanding how behaviors occur and how they can be influenced. According to the FBM, behavior happens when three elements converge simultaneously: **Motivation**, **Ability**, and **Prompt**. If any one of these elements is missing, the behavior is unlikely to occur.

1. Motivation: The "Why" Behind Behavior

Motivation is the driving force behind any action. It can be intrinsic (e.g., personal values, satisfaction) or extrinsic (e.g., rewards, recognition). Understanding what motivates individuals is essential for designing interventions that align with their needs and priorities.

Motivating Change in a Financial Institution A Fortune 50 bank struggled to adopt a customer-first approach in its retail banking division. Employees were hesitant to shift their focus, citing the anti-story, "We can't afford to prioritize personalization over efficiency." Leadership reframed this narrative, emphasizing how customer-centricity drove long-term profitability and aligned with employee values like trust and impact. By highlighting real stories of customers who benefited from personalized service, they motivated teams to prioritize this behavior.

Design Insight:

- Identify what motivates your audience. Are they driven by personal growth, recognition, or alignment with organizational values?

- Tailor interventions to connect with these motivations.

2. Ability: Making Behavior Feasible

Even the most motivated individuals will struggle to act if the behavior feels too difficult. Simplifying processes, removing barriers, and providing the right tools are critical for increasing ability.

Simplifying Sustainability Practices in a Global Retail Chain A global retail chain sought to reduce waste across its stores but faced resistance due to the perceived complexity of implementing eco-friendly practices. Leadership simplified the process by introducing user-friendly recycling guidelines and centralized waste management tools. Training sessions and clear visual aids helped employees feel confident in adopting these behaviors.

Design Insight:

- Ask: "What's making this behavior hard to do?"

- Simplify steps, provide resources, or automate repetitive tasks to make the behavior easier.

3. Prompt: The Catalyst for Action

Prompts are the triggers that remind individuals to take action. Without a well-timed and relevant prompt, even motivated and capable individuals may fail to act. Prompts can be external (e.g., notifications, visual cues) or internal (e.g., feelings, habits).

Using Digital Prompts to Boost Collaboration A Fortune 50 tech company introduced an internal collaboration platform but struggled with adoption. Leadership added automated prompts, such as reminders to share weekly updates and suggestions for relevant team connections. These well-timed prompts aligned with employees' existing workflows, driving consistent engagement.

Design Insight:

- Design prompts that are visible, timely, and directly connected to the desired behavior.

- Test different types of prompts (e.g., digital reminders, visual aids) to see what works best for your audience.

The Three Elements of Behavior Change

Elements of Fogg's Behavior Model

The Intersection of Motivation, Ability, and Prompt

The FBM emphasizes that these three elements must align for a behavior to occur. For example:

- **Motivation and Ability:** If motivation is high but the behavior feels too difficult, it won't happen.

- **Motivation and Prompt:** If motivation and ability are present but there's no reminder, the opportunity to act is lost.

Case Study: Driving DEI Initiatives with FBM in a Global Tech Firm

A global tech firm sought to embed inclusive hiring practices across its operations. The FBM revealed key gaps:

1. Motivation: Employees saw inclusion as important but were unsure how it applied to their roles.

2. Ability: Managers lacked training in inclusive hiring techniques.

3. Prompt: Recruitment systems didn't surface DEI-focused reminders during the hiring process.

Interventions Designed:

- Motivation: Leadership emphasized how inclusion drove innovation and team success.

- Ability: Created micro-learning modules to upskill managers in inclusive practices.

- Prompt: Added DEI-focused nudges in the hiring platform, such as reminders to review diverse candidate pools.

Outcome: Within one year, the firm achieved a 15% increase in diverse hires and improved employee sentiment around inclusion by 20%.

Reflection for Readers:

- Are your teams motivated to perform the desired behavior?

- Have you removed obstacles to make the behavior easier?

- Do you have clear and timely prompts to trigger the behavior?

Aligning Interventions with the Reframed Mindset

Behavioral change succeeds when it aligns with the beliefs and narratives established during the **Reframe** phase of the Catalyst Framework. Without this alignment, even well-designed interventions can fail to resonate, leaving teams disengaged or reverting to old habits.

Imagine an organization that publicly commits to fostering innovation but penalizes teams for failure. This misalignment between the reframed mindset ("Innovation requires risk-taking") and operational practices undermines trust and stifles experimentation. Alignment ensures that the reframed mindset is embedded into actions, systems, and culture, making it an integral part of the transformation journey.

Why Alignment Matters

Effective alignment bridges the gap between mindset and action by ensuring that:

1. **Systems Support the Narrative:** Policies, processes, and tools must reinforce the new belief.

2. **Behaviors Model the Mindset:** Leaders and teams must exemplify the desired behaviors.

3. **Recognition Rewards Alignment:** Incentives and feedback should celebrate actions that reflect the reframed narrative.

Case Study: Fostering Risk-Taking in Financial Services

Scenario:

A financial services firm shifted its narrative from "Failure is a threat" to "Failure is an opportunity for growth." However, initial efforts to encourage risk-taking were undercut by a lingering blame culture where mistakes were met with criticism.

Interventions Designed:

1. **Workshops on Failure:** Teams participated in sessions analyzing past mistakes to identify lessons learned, normalizing failure as part of growth.

2. **Risk-Reward Incentives:** Leadership introduced rewards for bold initiatives, even if they didn't succeed, to promote experimentation.

3. **Success Stories:** Managers highlighted examples where calculated risks led to breakthroughs, showcasing the benefits of taking chances.

Outcome:

Within a year, the firm saw a 25% increase in innovative initiatives. Employee surveys reflected higher psychological safety, with teams reporting greater confidence in experimenting without fear of blame.

Strategies for Building Alignment Through Behavioral Design

1. Translate the Narrative into Specific Behaviors

Break down the reframed narrative into actionable and measurable behaviors.

Example:

A company shifting from *"Customers are transactions"* to *"Customers are partners"* introduced a new behavior: asking clients during meetings, "What's one thing we can improve for you?"

2. Redesign Systems to Reflect the New Belief

Ensure that tools, workflows, and policies reinforce the desired behaviors.

Example:

A retail chain reframed its narrative to prioritize sustainability. To align with this mindset, procurement policies were updated to favor eco-friendly suppliers, reinforcing the belief through everyday operations.

3. Embed the Mindset into Rituals and Routines

Daily and weekly practices can anchor the reframed narrative, ensuring consistency across teams.

Example:

A manufacturing firm transitioning to a growth mindset began each meeting with a "Lessons Learned" segment, fostering reflection and normalizing failure as part of the learning process.

Case Study: Embedding Customer-Centricity in Healthcare

Scenario:

A healthcare organization shifted from "We know what's best for patients" to "Patients are partners in their care." This reframed mindset required cultural and operational alignment.

Interventions Designed:

1. **Patient Feedback Loops:** Surveys and focus groups were introduced to capture patients' voices, reinforcing the narrative of partnership.

2. **Training Programs:** Staff attended workshops on empathetic communication and active listening.

3. **Recognition for Patient Advocacy:** Employees who demonstrated patient-first care were celebrated during town halls.

Outcome:

The organization improved patient satisfaction scores by 30% and reduced complaints by 15% within two years, proving the power of aligning systems with the reframed mindset.

Reflection for Readers

- Do your systems, policies, and behaviors reflect the reframed narratives, or are there misalignments?

- What rituals, routines, or recognition programs could reinforce the new mindset?

- ***THIS SECTION IS STILL TO BE DONE***

Reinforcing Change Through Behavioral Design

Reinforcement is the cornerstone of lasting behavioral change. Without reinforcement, new behaviors risk becoming fleeting efforts rather than embedded practices. Leaders must create systems that ensure changes stick, transforming them into adaptive, lasting behaviors.

The Catalyst Framework's Design phase focuses on translating reframed narratives into actionable behaviors that drive transformation. By leveraging repetition, reinforcement, and exposure, organizations can embed these behaviors into their culture and ensure they become the default way of working.

The Role of Repetition in Building Habits

Repetition strengthens neural pathways—the more frequently a behavior is practiced, the more natural it becomes. In an organizational context, repetition ensures that new ways of working shift from conscious effort to habitual action.

Example: Embedding Customer-Centricity in Telecom

A telecom company encouraged frontline employees to ask every customer, *"What's one thing we can do better for you?"* This simple, repeatable behavior became a daily practice, embedding customer-centricity into the company's culture. Over time, this small act led to a 20% improvement in customer satisfaction scores and strengthened the company's reputation for responsiveness.

Design Insight for Repetition:

- Identify a single, repeatable behavior that aligns with the reframed mindset and integrate it into daily workflows.

- Make the behavior easy to practice by removing friction and supporting consistency.

- Celebrate small wins to reinforce positive behavior.

Reinforcement: Strengthening New Pathways

New behaviors stick when they are consistently reinforced through recognition, storytelling, and incentives. Leaders must ensure that the desired behaviors are linked to positive feedback and organizational values so they become ingrained in the culture.

Example: Recognizing Collaborative Wins in Healthcare

A healthcare organization transitioning to team-based care celebrated collaborative efforts through a peer recognition program. Teams that worked together to improve patient outcomes were highlighted in weekly meetings and newsletters. This consistent reinforcement strengthened the culture of collaboration and improved patient outcomes by 15%.

Practical Tips for Reinforcement:

1. Recognize Successes: Publicly acknowledge behaviors that align with the reframed mindset.

    - Example: Recognize teams that experiment with new ideas, even if the outcomes are mixed.

2. Share Stories: Use storytelling to illustrate the positive impact of new behaviors.

    - Example: Share how a new initiative helped a customer or improved efficiency.

3. Provide Tangible Rewards: Align incentives with the desired behavior.

   ○ Example: Offer bonuses or career advancement opportunities for teams that embrace change.

Exposure: Challenging Entrenched Patterns

In addition to repetition and reinforcement, exposure to new experiences helps challenge entrenched patterns and expand perspectives. This might include engaging with other teams, industries, or customers to see challenges from a new angle. Exposure encourages adaptation by broadening individuals' and teams' horizons, helping them envision new possibilities that were previously unconsidered.

Example: Breaking Down Silos Through Job Swapping

A logistics firm encouraged exposure by implementing a cross-departmental job-swapping program. Employees from operations spent a week in customer service, while sales team members shadowed warehouse staff. This exposure broadened understanding, challenged siloed thinking, and fostered empathy across departments.

Design Insight for Exposure:

- Create opportunities for employees to engage with diverse perspectives, such as cross-functional projects, job shadowing, or external benchmarking visits.

- Regularly expose teams to innovative practices or solutions outside of their immediate context to inspire new ways of thinking.

Case Study: Rewiring Risk-Taking Through Reinforcement

Scenario:

A financial services firm sought to embed the mindset, *"Failure fuels growth,"* into its culture. However, employees were hesitant to take risks, fearing repercussions for failure.

Interventions Designed:

1. Structured Reflection on Failures: Monthly "Lessons Learned" forums provided a safe space to analyze unsuccessful projects.

2. Leadership Role Modeling: Senior leaders shared their own stories of failure and how they turned setbacks into opportunities.

3. Recognition for Experimentation: Teams that demonstrated creativity and resilience, even in failed attempts, were celebrated during company-wide events.

Outcome:

Within a year, employees reported a 40% increase in psychological safety, and the organization launched multiple innovative projects, two of which became market leaders.

Reflection for Readers:

- What behaviors in your organization need reinforcement to become lasting habits?

- How might repetition, reinforcement, or exposure accelerate the embedding of new behaviors?

Just as neuroplasticity rewires the brain through repetition and reinforcement, organizations must create structured environments that support and sustain behavior change over time. By embedding desired behaviors into daily workflows, leadership practices, and cultural norms, transformation becomes not just an initiative—but an enduring capability.

Practical Framework for Designing Behavioural Change

Reframing anti-stories sets the foundation for transformation, but for true change to take hold, behaviors must be intentionally designed and reinforced. This five-step framework ensures that new mindsets lead to tangible actions, using structured interventions that make behavioral change repeatable and sustainable..

Step 1: Identify the Desired Behavior

The first step is to clearly define the behavior you want to encourage. The more specific and measurable the behavior, the easier it will be to design interventions and assess their effectiveness.

Example:

- **Behavior:** "Managers will provide constructive feedback to each team member during weekly one-on-one meetings."

- **Measurable Outcome:** Increased employee engagement scores and improved performance reviews.

Design Insight:

- **What specific behavior aligns with your reframed mindset?**

- **How will success be measured?**

  - Define success metrics in terms of tangible outcomes (e.g., productivity, employee engagement, or customer satisfaction).

Step 2: Apply the Fogg Behavior Model

Once the behavior is identified, evaluate the behavior using the Fogg Behavior Model (FBM) to ensure that all elements—**motivation, ability**, and **prompt**—are addressed. If any of these elements are missing, the behavior is unlikely to happen.

Questions to Apply the FBM:

- **Motivation:** Why should individuals want to perform this behavior? What incentives or values can you highlight?

  - Example: Highlight how feedback improves team performance and individual growth.

- **Ability:** What barriers make this behavior difficult? How can you simplify the process?

  - Example: Provide managers with a simple feedback framework or template to guide them.

- **Prompt:** What cues or reminders will trigger the behavior at the right time?

  - Example: Schedule weekly reminders on managers' calendars to ensure the behavior occurs consistently.

Design Insight:

- Ensure that the **motivation** behind the behavior is clear and appealing, making it meaningful to the individuals or teams involved.

- **Simplify the behavior** to make it as easy as possible to implement and practice.

- Use **well-timed prompts** to trigger the desired behavior, creating consistent cues that trigger action.

Step 3: Design the Intervention

The next step is to design an intervention that aligns with the desired behavior, Fogg's model, and the reframed mindset. The intervention should be structured to reduce friction and encourage action.

Design Elements to Consider:

- **Tools:** Create templates, checklists, or dashboards to simplify actions.

- **Processes:** Establish clear workflows or protocols to make the behavior routine.

- **Systems:** Align incentives, recognition, and performance metrics with the desired behavior.

Example: Driving Cross-Functional Collaboration

- **Tools:** Introduced collaboration software with predefined workflows for cross-team projects.

- **Processes:** Scheduled biweekly check-ins for cross-functional teams to ensure consistent progress.

- **Systems:** Established shared KPIs to align departmental goals with broader organizational outcomes.

Design Insight:

- What systems, tools, or processes can you create to reduce friction and ensure the desired behavior occurs?

- Ensure that the systems you design reinforce the behavior in a seamless and continuous manner.

Step 4: Test and Iterate

Now that the intervention is designed, it's time to pilot it. Testing allows you to refine your approach before scaling it across the organization. Use feedback to make necessary adjustments and build confidence in the effectiveness of the intervention.

Steps for Testing:

1. **Select a Representative Pilot Group:** Choose a team or department to test the intervention. This should be a group that represents the broader population but is small enough to allow for manageable testing.

2. **Define Metrics:** Set clear success metrics (e.g., adoption rates, engagement levels) to track the progress and effectiveness of the intervention.

3. **Gather Feedback:** Collect both qualitative and quantitative feedback to identify strengths and areas for improvement.

Example: Testing a New Onboarding Program

- **Pilot Group:** A department within the company that struggles with onboarding effectiveness.

- **Metrics:** Measure training completion rates, feedback quality, and time-to-productivity for new hires.

- **Feedback:** Gather input from new employees on how to improve the onboarding experience.

Design Insight:

- How will you measure success during the pilot phase?

- How will you use feedback to refine the intervention before scaling it?

Step 5: Scale and Embed Behavioral Change

Once the intervention has been successfully tested and refined, the next step is to scale it across the organization. Scaling requires not just reinforcement but embedding the behavior into systems, processes, and leadership routines to make it self-sustaining.

Scaling Strategies:

1. **Codify the New Behavior**: Integrate the behavior into standard workflows, policies, or training programs.

   Example: A retail company made sustainability practices part of its employee onboarding process.

2. **Create Structural Reinforcement**: Ensure systems, KPIs, and incentives align with the behavior change.

   Example: A financial firm linked knowledge-sharing to performance reviews.

3. **Empower Champions:** Identify early adopters and equip them to coach others, turning behavior change into a movement.

   Example: A healthcare organization appointed "collaboration champions" to mentor new team members in cross-functional teamwork.

Example: Scaling Sustainability Practices in Retail

- Recognition: Celebrate early adopters of sustainable practices, such as reducing waste in stores.

- Integration: Align sustainability goals with performance metrics to reinforce the behavior.

Design Insight:

- How will you scale the intervention across teams or departments?

- What strategies will you use to ensure that the behavior is reinforced continuously?

Case Study: Designing Behavioral Change in Financial Services

Scenario:

A financial services firm sought to increase knowledge-sharing across teams to improve decision-making. However, silos and competing priorities hindered collaboration.

Intervention Designed:

1. **Behavior Identified**: "Team members will share one key insight from their projects during weekly all-hands meetings."

2. **FBM Applied:**

   - **Motivation**: Leadership highlighted how shared insights led to better outcomes in other teams.

   - **Ability**: Created a template for sharing insights in under five minutes.

   - **Prompt:** Sent calendar invites with reminders before meetings.

3. **Pilot Program**: Tested the approach with one team and gathered feedback to refine the template.

4. **Reinforcement**: Recognized contributors in monthly newsletters.

5. **Scaling**: Expanded the practice across departments after successful results.

Outcome:

Knowledge-sharing increased by 50%, improving cross-departmental collaboration and decision-making quality.

Designing behavior change is only the beginning. Once new behaviors are embedded into workflows, they must be executed at scale with consistency and accountability. In the next chapter, Execute, we will explore how to drive momentum, maintain adaptability, and ensure behavior change is sustained in real-world environments.

Chapter Summary

- The Design phase of the Catalyst Framework turns reframed narratives into repeatable behaviors by applying behavioral science, systems thinking, and neuroplasticity principles.

- Inspired by Fogg's Behavior Model (FBM), effective behavior change occurs when Motivation, Ability, and Prompt align:

- Motivation – Connects behaviors to intrinsic or extrinsic drivers (e.g., purpose, recognition).

- Ability – Simplifies behaviors by removing complexity and friction.

- Prompt – Uses timely, visible cues to trigger action at the right moment.

- Behavioral interventions must be **aligned with the reframed mindset** to ensure credibility and long-term cultural adoption.

- Repetition, reinforcement, and exposure are essential to embedding behaviors and rewiring default organizational habits.

- Strategies for embedding behavior include:

  - **Translating narratives into specific behaviors** (e.g., asking customers "How can we improve?").

  - **Redesigning systems and policies** to reinforce those behaviors (e.g., shared KPIs or sustainability-linked procurement).

  - **Embedding routines** (e.g., "Lessons Learned" segments in team meetings).

- A 5-step framework supports sustainable behavioral change:

  - Identify the behavior

  - Apply FBM

- ○ Design the intervention

- ○ Test and iterate

- ○ Scale and embed

- Case studies throughout the chapter show how behavior design led to measurable results in areas like DEI, customer-centricity, innovation, and cross-functional collaboration.

Design is the bridge between belief and execution. When done well, it transforms mindset into movement—and rituals into culture.

Action Exercises

1. Behavior Mapping Exercise

Objective: Apply the **Fogg Behavior Model (FBM)** to map and design a behavior change intervention in your organization.

Steps:

1. **Identify the desired behavior.**

   - *Example:* "Employees will contribute to a knowledge-sharing platform weekly."

2. **Apply the FBM:**

   - *Motivation: Emphasize how knowledge-sharing benefits team efficiency.*

   - *Ability: Simplify the process by creating templates or auto-reminders.*

   - *Prompt:* Use calendar invites or platform notifications as triggers.

3. **Design the intervention** and **implement it with one team** as a test.

4. Track adoption rates and gather feedback to refine the approach.

2. Pilot an Intervention

Objective: Test a small-scale intervention to ensure feasibility before scaling.

Steps:

1. **Select a team or department** to pilot the intervention.

2. **Define clear metrics** to track success (**e.g., participation rates, feedback quality**).

3. **Run the pilot for a fixed period** (e.g., two weeks).

4. **Debrief participants** to evaluate effectiveness and identify areas for improvement.

Example:

A company piloted a **peer recognition program** where employees submitted weekly shout-outs for team members. After tracking participation and impact on morale, the program was expanded organization-wide.

3. Design a Recognition System for Behavior Reinforcement

Objective: Reinforce a key behavior in your organization by **designing a structured recognition system.**

Steps:

1. **Define the behavior** to be recognized (**e.g., collaboration, creativity, customer-centricity**).

2. **Establish clear recognition criteria** to ensure fairness and consistency.

3. Select platforms for reinforcement (e.g., newsletters, town halls, digital dashboards).

4. Monitor the program's impact on engagement and behavior repetition.

Example:

A healthcare organization introduced a **"Teamwork Spotlight"** feature in their weekly newsletter, showcasing teams that collaborated on challenging cases. This reinforced the **importance of collaboration**, inspiring other teams to adopt similar practices.

4. Leadership Behavior Change Challenge

Objective: Apply **behavior design principles** to a leadership behavior you want to improve in your team.

Steps:

1. **Identify a leadership behavior** that will positively influence your team's culture.

   - *Example:* "Managers will hold weekly check-ins focused on team well-being and professional growth."

2. **Apply the FBM:**

   - **Motivation:** Highlight how regular check-ins improve engagement and retention.

   - **Ability:** Provide managers with a simple one-page check-in guide.

   - **Prompt:** Schedule automated calendar reminders for all managers.

3. **Run the new practice for one month** and collect feedback from employees.

4. **Refine based on feedback** and plan for organization-wide adoption.

5. Knowledge-Sharing Challenge

Objective: Foster a culture of collaboration by encouraging teams to share insights and best practices.

Steps:

1. **Set up a shared platform** (Slack, internal wiki, email digest) where employees can contribute insights.

2. **Schedule weekly prompts** in team meetings or emails to encourage participation.

3. **Recognize top contributors** by featuring them in company communications.

Example:

A tech company asked employees to share **one learning from their week** on a shared Slack channel. By reinforcing contributions with **leadership feedback**, knowledge-sharing increased **by 40% in six months.**

Reflection for Readers

- Which of these exercises aligns best with your organization's behavioral change goals?

- How might **small-scale pilots or recognition programs** help sustain new behaviors over time?

- What leadership-driven behaviors could you reinforce in your team today?

Chapter 10:

Execute: Translating Strategy into Action

Execution is where the rubber meets the road, where transformation plans evolve from theoretical blueprints to tangible outcomes. In the Catalyst Framework, the **Execute phase** serves as the bridge that connects strategy to measurable results. It's the phase where behaviors, systems, and actions converge, bringing transformation to life.

Imagine a symphony. Every musician holds a part of the score, yet without the conductor guiding them, the music would remain silent. Similarly, no matter how perfectly designed a transformation strategy may be, without disciplined execution, it risks remaining unrealized potential. Execution is the conductor that aligns the players and ensures every note leads toward the intended harmony. **But unlike a symphony, execution in the Catalyst Framework is iterative**, continuously refined based on feedback, ensuring alignment with transformation goals.

The **Execute phase** is distinct because it doesn't just call for action; it prioritizes **aligned and iterative action**. It connects the reframed mindset from the Reframe phase to concrete behaviors and systems that drive lasting change. Execution requires not just the initiation of new actions but also ongoing reflection and adaptation to ensure continuous momentum and success.

Reflection for Readers:

- Think about a transformation effort you've led or experienced. Were the execution steps clearly defined and aligned with the overarching goals?

- How might a structured, iterative approach to execution improve your current or future initiatives?

What Makes Execution Different in the Catalyst Framework?

Execution in the Catalyst Framework is not just about completing tasks—it's about **aligning every action with the reframed mindsets and transformation goals** established in the earlier phases. The power of execution lies in **its ability to adapt and evolve** as feedback is gathered, ensuring that transformation efforts remain relevant and impactful.

Here's what sets the Execute phase apart:

1. **It Embeds the Transformation Mindset**: Every action is designed to reinforce the new narratives and behaviors. Instead of merely applying old methods in a new context, execution in the Catalyst Framework **integrates the transformation mindset** into daily actions, ensuring alignment with the growth-oriented beliefs developed in the **Reframe** phase.

2. **It Is Iterative**: Unlike traditional models, where execution is a one-time event, the **Execute phase** in the Catalyst Framework is iterative. Teams constantly assess their actions, learn from outcomes, and refine their strategies to stay aligned with transformation goals. **Execution is a process of continuous improvement**, where feedback loops from both internal and external sources help **adapt interventions in real time**.

3. **It Focuses on Systems, Not Just Tasks**: Execution isn't just about ticking off tasks. It's about designing systems and structures that integrate new behaviors into **organizational culture**, making transformation a sustainable way of working. This systems-focused approach ensures that change isn't temporary—it becomes ingrained in the fabric of the organization.

Execution in the Catalyst Framework is about creating an environment where new behaviors are **continuously tested, adjusted, and reinforced**, ensuring that transformation is sustained and scalable over time.

Reflection for Readers:

- Are the actions your teams are taking clearly aligned with the reframed mindset and transformation goals?

- How might adopting an iterative approach to execution help refine and improve your current transformation initiatives?

Key Goals of the Execute Phase

The Execute phase is where transformation efforts are tested, refined, and brought to life. The success of this phase depends on the alignment of actions, behaviors, and systems with the reframed mindsets established in earlier stages. The four key goals of the Execute phase are as follows:

1. Translate Strategy into Action: Execution is where plans become tangible. It's not enough to have a strategy—you must ensure that it has a clear path to implementation. This involves breaking down strategic objectives into actionable steps, assigning responsibilities, and setting clear, measurable outcomes. Clarity in execution allows teams to understand not just what they need to do, but how their actions will drive transformation.

2. Foster Accountability: Ownership and accountability are essential for the success of any transformation. Clear roles and responsibilities ensure that everyone knows what they are responsible for. In the Catalyst Framework, every intervention is assigned a designated owner who is accountable for its completion. This sense of accountability empowers individuals and teams to act decisively and stay committed to the transformation process.

3. Reinforce New Behaviors: New behaviors must be continuously practiced to become ingrained in the organization. Repetition and reinforcement are key to making these behaviors second nature. Leaders and teams should regularly revisit the behaviors they want to see, ensuring that actions are aligned with the reframed mindset and transformation goals. Reinforcing positive

actions through feedback, recognition, and incentives helps embed new behaviors into daily routines.

4. Adapt and Align: Execution is not static. As you move through the transformation, feedback loops provide real-time insights into what's working and what's not. The Execute phase relies on adaptation—teams must be able to tweak strategies and interventions based on the feedback they receive. This ensures that the transformation stays aligned with the evolving needs of the organization, its people, and the external environment.

The Execute phase is the turning point where vision and strategy come together in meaningful, aligned actions. It's where transformation starts to take shape and becomes real, measurable change. However, for execution to be truly effective, it must be seen as an iterative process, constantly improving and evolving to meet the needs of the organization and its people.

Reflection for Readers:

- Are the actions you're taking clearly aligned with the reframed mindset and transformation goals?

- How can feedback loops and iterative execution help you adapt strategies and drive continuous improvement?

Best Practices for Driving Implementation and Accountability

The execution of transformation efforts requires discipline, structure, and a shared sense of ownership across all levels of the organization. Successful execution hinges on the following best practices:

1. Align Execution with the Reframed Mindset

Execution must always reflect the **reframed mindset developed in the Reframe phase**. Actions should consistently support the new narratives established around behaviors and beliefs. If the mindset has shifted—for instance, from **"Innovation is risky" to "Innovation**

is essential for growth"—the execution efforts should prioritize **experimentation, risk-taking, and collaboration.**

Example: Embedding a Learning Culture in Pharma

A **pharmaceutical company** reframed its anti-story from *"Failure is unacceptable"* to *"Failure is a learning opportunity."* To embed this into execution, they:

- Introduced **innovation sprints**, where teams developed prototypes in **short cycles**.

- Created **structured reflection forums**, where even unsuccessful ideas were **analyzed for insights**.

- Celebrated **learning-based successes** to reinforce the new execution mindset.

Practical Tip: Regularly check to ensure that **each intervention aligns with the reframed narrative.** Ask: *Does this reinforce or contradict the transformation story we're telling?*

2. Establish Ownership at Every Level

Clear ownership ensures that responsibilities are well-defined, driving accountability. In the Catalyst Framework, every action or intervention should have a designated owner who is **responsible** for its execution and **accountable** for its results. This helps ensure that action is not just taken, but **driven with purpose**.

Tool: RACI Matrix The **RACI Matrix** is a practical tool for clarifying roles and ensuring accountability:

1. **Responsible:** Who performs the task?

2. **Accountable:** Who ensures the task is completed?

3. **Consulted:** Who provides input or expertise?

4. **Informed:** Who needs updates on progress?

Example: A telecom company transitioning to a **customer-first** culture assigned "Customer Experience Ambassadors" in each department to ensure execution aligned with the company's goals by monitoring progress and providing feedback.

Practical Tip: Use tools like **Trello**, **Asana**, or **Microsoft Teams** to visually track responsibilities and ensure alignment across teams.

3. Start Small and Scale Strategically

To reduce risk and build confidence, start with small, manageable interventions or pilot programs. **Pilot projects** allow organizations to test the effectiveness of their plans before rolling them out on a larger scale. This iterative process reduces uncertainty and provides valuable feedback that can be used to refine interventions.

Example: A logistics firm piloted a **digital tracking system** in one region before scaling it globally. The feedback from the pilot allowed them to address challenges and adjust the system, ensuring a smoother global rollout.

Practical Tip: Choose a pilot group that represents your organization's **diversity**—considering factors like **geography, department, and role**—so the feedback will be as comprehensive as possible.

4. Integrate Actions into Daily Workflows

For execution to succeed, new behaviors **must not feel like extra work.** Embedding execution into **existing processes and daily work routines** ensures long-term adoption.

Example: A tech company introduced a **"Daily Huddle"** ritual where teams reviewed their goals and discussed progress. This simple practice reinforced alignment with transformation objectives and became a natural part of the workday, without adding complexity.

Practical Tip: Design interventions that **feel seamless** within current workflows. Frame new behaviors as part of normal operations, rather than as additional tasks.

5. Use Clear Metrics to Track Progress

The effectiveness of any transformation effort must be measured. Establish **clear and actionable metrics** that are aligned with transformation goals.

These metrics help provide direction, track progress, and **highlight areas for improvement.**

Example: A retail chain transitioning to a **sustainability-first** mindset tracked key metrics, such as **waste reduction**, **employee participation in green initiatives**, and **customer perceptions** of eco-friendly practices.

Practical Tip: Use **SMART** goals (Specific, Measurable, Achievable, Relevant, Time-bound) to define clear targets for each intervention. Continuously measure and assess these metrics to ensure alignment with the overarching goals of the transformation.

Reflection for Readers

- Are your **execution plans** clearly aligned with the reframed mindset and transformation goals?

- Does every intervention have a **clear owner** and **defined success metrics**?

- How can you integrate **new actions** into daily routines to make them **sustainable**?

The Role of Feedback Loops in Execution

Feedback loops are the backbone of effective execution. They provide continuous insights into what is working, what needs adjustment, and where to refine the strategy. In the Catalyst Framework, feedback loops are instrumental in ensuring that execution remains aligned with transformation goals and allows for iterative improvement.

Feedback loops serve three critical purposes:

1. **Continuous Improvement**: Feedback allows teams to make ongoing refinements, adapting their approaches based on real-time insights.

2. **Reinforcement of Mindsets**: They highlight successes and areas of progress, reinforcing the transformation mindset.

3. **Alignment with Goals:** Feedback ensures that actions and behaviors remain in line with the organization's vision, values, and strategic objectives.

Feedback loops can be both internal (focused on team reflections) and external (drawing insights from stakeholders or customers), offering a holistic system for monitoring and adapting execution efforts.

1. Internal Feedback Loops

Internal feedback loops focus on gathering insights from within the organization. They provide teams with the opportunity to reflect on their progress, share what's working, and identify areas for improvement. These loops are essential for creating transparency, maintaining alignment, and fostering a growth mindset.

Example: Engineering Team Retrospectives

An engineering firm introduced **biweekly retrospectives**, where teams answered the following questions:

- What went well?

- What didn't go well?

- What can we improve?

This practice fostered transparency, strengthened collaboration, and helped the team adjust their execution strategy to stay aligned with their goals.

Practical Tools for Internal Feedback Loops:

- **Team Check-Ins**: Regular, short meetings to review progress and address obstacles.

- **Digital Platforms**: Tools like **Slack** or **Microsoft Teams** to quickly gather input from team members.

- **Reflection Templates**: Structured templates to guide team discussions on performance and alignment.

2. External Feedback Loops

External feedback loops gather insights from outside the organization. This includes feedback from customers, stakeholders, or the broader market. These loops ensure that the execution efforts are resonating with those outside the organization and that the strategy remains relevant and effective.

Example: Customer Surveys in Sustainability Initiatives

A consumer goods company executing a **sustainability program** used customer feedback through **online surveys** to gather insights on their preferences for eco-friendly packaging. These insights informed adjustments to the program, enhancing its effectiveness and market appeal.

Practical Tools for External Feedback Loops:

- **Net Promoter Score (NPS)**: A tool to gauge customer loyalty and satisfaction.

- **Stakeholder Interviews**: Qualitative insights gathered from key stakeholders.

- **Social Media Listening**: Monitoring online conversations to identify feedback and trends related to initiatives.

3. Tools for Feedback Loops

Implementing effective feedback loops requires the right tools to collect, analyze, and act on data. Below are key tools that can help implement internal and external feedback loops:

- **Progress Dashboards**: These provide real-time insights into key metrics and milestones.

   - **Example**: A sales team tracks weekly progress toward targets using a **live dashboard**, allowing quick course corrections.

- **Pulse Surveys**: These quick surveys gather employee or customer feedback on specific initiatives.

   - **Example**: A tech company uses **pulse surveys** to assess employee confidence during a major process overhaul.

- **Reflection Sessions**: These meetings foster open discussions about successes, challenges, and learnings.

   - **Example**: A nonprofit hosts **monthly "Reflection Fridays"**, where teams share impact stories and discuss areas for growth.

Case Study: Feedback Loops in a Retail Transformation

Scenario: A retail chain transitioning to a **digital-first strategy** relied heavily on feedback loops to ensure smooth execution.

Approach:

1. **Internal Feedback**: Weekly team meetings reviewed metrics such as **adoption rates for new digital tools** and **customer wait times** in stores.

2. **External Feedback**: Customer surveys and **focus groups** provided insights on user experiences with the retailer's new mobile app.

3. **Refinements**: Based on feedback, the app's interface was simplified, and additional training sessions were provided for store employees.

Outcome: Customer satisfaction scores increased by 25%, and app adoption rates exceeded projections within six months.

Reflection for Readers

- Are your **feedback loops** providing actionable insights that drive improvement?

- How can you balance **internal** and **external feedback** to ensure a comprehensive understanding of your execution efforts?

Reinforcing the Rewired Mindset Through Repetition

Execution is not just about completing tasks—it's about making behaviors automatic and deeply ingrained in daily operations. Organizations sustain transformation by designing structured routines, check-ins, and milestone-driven execution plans that ensure behaviors don't fade over time.

When organizations consistently repeat and reinforce desired behaviors, they create a feedback loop that builds momentum, increases confidence, and solidifies the transformation mindset. This process is fundamental to ensuring that new behaviors stick and become ingrained in the organizational culture.

Why Repetition in Execution Matters

Organizations must ensure that new behaviors are not only practiced but **consistently reinforced and measured** to prevent regression.

1. **Strengthening New Pathways**: Repeated actions build familiarity and ease, making new behaviors feel natural. The more consistently a behavior is executed, the more deeply ingrained it becomes.

2. **Preventing Regression**: Without structured reinforcement, **old habits and behaviors resurface**, undermining transformation efforts. Execution ensures that behaviors **do not fade** by integrating them into governance structures, reporting mechanisms, and team-level accountability.

Example: Embedding Agility in a Retail Chain

A **retail company** transitioning to **an omnichannel business model** used execution-driven repetition to embed agility into its operations.

- **Daily Stand-Ups**: Teams discussed goals and challenges in **quick, focused meetings**.

- **Weekly Reflections**: eams reviewed progress, celebrated wins, and identified areas for improvement.

- **Leadership Reinforcement**: Early successes were highlighted in newsletters and town halls to showcase agility as a **core company value**.

Outcome: Over time, these repeated practices **rewired the organization's culture**, embedding agility as a **standard operating behavior**.

Execution Strategies for Reinforcing Behaviors Through Repetition

1. Daily Rituals for Execution Consistency

Simple, repeatable **execution-driven routines** ensure that transformation goals remain active and visible. These rituals should be easy to integrate into existing workflows and should feel like a natural part of the team's day-to-day operations.

Example: Driving Execution Focus in Sales Teams

A sales team introduced a 10-minute morning huddle to:

- Align on key performance priorities.

- Share insights from client conversations.

- Reinforce sales execution best practices.

Execution Tip: Structure execution routines so they are **embedded within normal operations** rather than positioned as additional workload.

2. Team-Based Execution Practices

Teams must share collective ownership for execution success. Shared team-level execution routines create accountability and ensure sustained behavioral reinforcement.

Example: Aligning Execution in Healthcare Teams

A healthcare organization shifting to a team-based care model introduced:

- Weekly Interdisciplinary Meetings – Doctors, nurses, and admin staff coordinated patient care.

- Joint Goal-Setting Reviews – Teams aligned on shared metrics for care outcomes.

Execution Tip: Team-based rituals foster collective accountability and prevent execution failures due to lack of ownership.

3. Organization-Wide Execution Milestones

Execution must be reinforced at the **organizational level** by integrating milestone-driven accountability and leadership visibility..

Example: Scaling Lean Execution in Manufacturing

A manufacturing company transitioning to lean operations used:

- Quarterly Efficiency Reviews – Teams tracked lean adoption progress.

- Milestone-Based Recognition – Leadership highlighted teams that hit lean transformation targets.

Execution Tip: Milestones should reinforce behaviors rather than just recognize outcomes. Ensure that execution progress is measured at both the team and organizational levels.

Execution-Driven Recognition and Rewards

Recognition should not be standalone praise—it must be integrated into execution tracking systems, performance reviews, and leadership visibility.

Example: Recognizing Sustainability Efforts

A global logistics firm transitioning to eco-friendly operations created an:

- **"Execution Excellence" Award** – Recognized teams that met sustainability KPIs.

- **Integration with OKRs** – Employees who demonstrated execution leadership in sustainability were considered for promotion opportunities.

Execution Tip: Ensure recognition is aligned with execution KPIs and tied to real business outcomes.

Case Study: Execution-Driven Repetition in Action

Scenario:

A financial institution aimed to shift its culture from risk aversion to innovation, reinforcing the narrative *"Failure fuels growth."*

Execution Interventions:

- Leadership Role Modeling – Senior leaders shared lessons from their own failures during execution check-ins.

- Innovation Hours – Teams hosted weekly execution-focused brainstorming sessions.

- Execution-Linked Recognition – Employees who executed new strategic initiatives were featured in a "Trailblazer Spotlight" program.

Outcome:

Within a year:

- The organization launched five new products inspired by execution-level brainstorming.

- Employee engagement scores rose by 15% due to increased execution confidence.

Reflection for Readers

- What execution routines can reinforce behaviors and sustain transformation?

- How might you use structured execution strategies to ensure behaviors remain embedded at scale?

- Where in your organization does execution break down, and how can structured routines improve discipline?

Case Study: Successful Execution of the Catalyst Framework

Challenge:

A global healthcare provider set out to improve patient outcomes by shifting from a siloed, task-oriented culture to a collaborative, patient-first model. Despite a clear strategy, execution was hindered by cultural resistance and departmental silos. Employees lacked a sense of shared ownership, making collaboration difficult to sustain.

Approach: Executing the Catalyst Framework

The healthcare provider applied the Catalyst Framework to address these challenges, moving systematically through each phase:

1. Analyze: Identifying the Knowing-Doing Gap

Through focus groups and surveys, the organization uncovered a critical gap:

Employees believed that patient outcomes were solely the responsibility of doctors, creating disengagement among support staff and administrative teams.

Silos between clinical and administrative departments created inefficiencies, delaying care coordination.

Key Insight:

The knowing-doing gap stemmed from a lack of shared accountability and collaboration across roles.

2. Reframe: Shifting the Narrative

The leadership team reframed the anti-story, "Patient outcomes are the responsibility of doctors", to "Everyone contributes to patient outcomes." This new narrative emphasized the interconnected roles of all employees, from front-line nurses to administrative staff.

Actions Taken:

Leadership shared stories highlighting how non-clinical roles, such as schedulers and billing staff, directly impacted patient experiences.

Town halls featured patient testimonials, reinforcing the importance of teamwork in achieving positive outcomes.

3. Design: Creating Aligned Interventions

To reinforce the reframed narrative, the organization designed interventions that encouraged collaboration and accountability.

Key Interventions:

Team-Based Care Protocols: Multidisciplinary teams were formed to manage patient care collaboratively. Each team included doctors, nurses, administrators, and support staff.

Shared Success Metrics: Teams were measured collectively on metrics like patient satisfaction, care quality, and timeliness.

Training Programs: Employees participated in workshops to build skills in communication, problem-solving, and collaborative decision-making.

4. Execute: Translating Strategy into Action

During the Execute phase, the healthcare provider put these interventions into practice, focusing on ownership, feedback, and repetition.

Execution Steps:

Ownership: Each multidisciplinary team was assigned a team leader responsible for coordinating efforts and ensuring alignment with patient-first goals.

Daily Huddles: Teams held brief daily meetings to align on priorities, discuss patient needs, and address any roadblocks.

Feedback Loops: Patient surveys and regular team check-ins provided real-time feedback to refine workflows and improve collaboration.

Outcome: Delivering Results

Within 18 months, the organization achieved transformative outcomes:

30% Improvement in Patient Satisfaction Scores: Patients reported feeling more valued and cared for, thanks to streamlined coordination and personalized attention.

15% Reduction in Care Errors: Better communication and shared accountability reduced missteps in patient care.

Increased Employee Engagement: Staff surveys revealed a 20% boost in engagement, as employees felt their contributions were recognized and impactful.

Key Takeaways from the Case Study

Align Execution with Mindset: When every intervention reinforced the reframed belief of shared accountability, transformation efforts gained momentum.

Use Real-Time Feedback: Continuous input from patients and teams enabled timely adjustments and sustained progress.

Reinforce Through Routine: Daily huddles and shared metrics turned collaboration into a daily habit, embedding it in the culture.

Reflection for Readers

- Where might team-based accountability and daily execution rituals drive stronger collaboration in your organization?

- How could you use real-time feedback loops to refine execution in your current initiatives?

- Which phase of the Catalyst Framework needs the most attention in your current transformation efforts?

Chapter Summary

- The **Execute phase** of the Catalyst Framework is where **strategy becomes behavior**—translating reframed mindsets into aligned, visible, and measurable actions.

- Unlike traditional execution models, Catalyst emphasizes **alignment, iteration, and reinforcement**. It's not about doing more; it's about **doing what matters, consistently and collaboratively.**

- The 4 core goals of execution are:

  1. **Translate strategy into action** – Break vision into clear, measurable steps.

  2. **Foster accountability** – Assign ownership at every level using tools like the RACI matrix.

  3. **Reinforce new behaviors** – Embed behaviors into workflows through daily routines and systems.

  4. **Adapt and align** – Use feedback loops to refine efforts in real-time and sustain progress.

- Execution succeeds when it is **integrated into daily work**, **tracked with clear metrics**, and **guided by real-time feedback** from both internal and external stakeholders.

- Key practices include:

  1. Starting small with pilots and scaling gradually.

  2. Aligning systems, policies, and recognition with the new mindset.

  3. Embedding daily rituals like huddles, reflections, or team-based reviews.

- Feedback loops—both internal (team retrospectives) and external (customer input)—are crucial to course-correct and stay aligned with transformation goals.

- Repetition and recognition reinforce behavior at scale. Without them, old habits return. With them, transformation becomes part of the culture.

- A detailed case study (healthcare transformation) illustrates how Catalyst execution improved collaboration, accountability, and patient outcomes through shared metrics, rituals, and consistent reinforcement.

Execute is where belief becomes behavior, and strategy becomes sustained momentum.

Action Exercises

The following exercises are designed to help leaders and teams apply the principles of execution and behavioral change to their own transformation initiatives. By practicing these steps, you can ensure that the strategies you've developed are translated into meaningful action and measurable outcomes.

1. Ownership Audit

Objective: Ensure that every task or initiative in your current transformation project has a clear owner and defined roles.

Steps:

1. Identify a transformation project or initiative.

2. List all tasks associated with the project.

3. Use a **RACI matrix** to assign roles:

   - **Responsible**: Who is performing the task?

   - **Accountable**: Who ensures the task is completed?

   - **Consulted**: Who provides input or expertise?

   - **Informed:** Who needs updates on progress?

4. Review the matrix with your team to ensure clarity and alignment.

Outcome: Improved accountability and streamlined execution.

2. Design a Feedback Loop

Objective: Create an internal or external feedback loop to monitor the progress of your transformation initiative.

Steps:

1. Choose a specific initiative (e.g., launching a new tool, improving customer satisfaction).

2. Define the type of feedback needed:

   ○ **Internal**: Team reflections, performance reviews.

   ○ **External:** Customer surveys, stakeholder interviews.

3. Select tools for collecting feedback (e.g., dashboards, pulse surveys, interviews).

4. Pilot the feedback loop over two weeks, gathering input and making adjustments.

Example: A tech team launching a new product uses customer feedback surveys to refine features and improve adoption rates.

3. Develop a Repetition Plan

Objective: Reinforce key behaviors critical to your transformation goals through repetition.

Steps:

1. Identify one critical behavior aligned with your transformation goals (e.g., daily collaboration, customer-first practices).

2. Create rituals or routines to practice this behavior regularly:

   ○ **Daily**: Morning huddles or status updates.

   ○ **Weekly**: Reflection sessions or progress reviews.

   ○ **Monthly:** Recognitions or celebrations of success.

3. Track progress over one month and adjust routines as needed to increase adoption.

Example: A healthcare organization improves patient care by conducting daily multidisciplinary team huddles.

4. Execute a Pilot Initiative

Objective: Test a small-scale version of a transformation initiative to refine and prepare for scaling.

Steps:

1. Define the scope of the pilot initiative and select a representative team or department to participate.

2. Identify clear success metrics to track during the pilot (e.g., efficiency gains, feedback quality).

3. Execute the pilot over a fixed period (e.g., one month).

4. Conduct a debrief to assess what worked, what didn't, and how to improve.

5. Refine the intervention based on feedback and prepare for organization-wide rollout.

Example: A logistics firm piloted a new tracking system in one region and gathered employee feedback to refine the system before global implementation.

5. Measure and Reflect

Objective: Track the progress of execution efforts and reflect on the results with your team.

Steps:

1. Identify key metrics to evaluate execution success (e.g., adoption rates, efficiency improvements, satisfaction scores).

2. Create a progress dashboard to visualize data in real-time.

3. Schedule regular reflection sessions to discuss progress, celebrate wins, and address challenges.

4. Document lessons learned and incorporate them into future execution plans.

Example: A retail chain tracks the adoption of a digital inventory system using a dashboard, adjusting training efforts based on regional performance data.

Reflection for Readers

- What behaviors or initiatives in your organization could benefit from the structured execution principles discussed in this chapter?

- How might feedback loops, repetition, and pilots improve your current execution strategies?

- Where can you apply small experiments this quarter to improve execution outcomes?

Chapter 11:

Making Change Stick: Sustaining the Transformation Mindset

Execution powers transformation, but sustainability ensures its longevity. Imagine planting a tree: the initial steps of selecting the right seed, preparing the soil, and watering it are crucial, but they are only the beginning. For the tree to grow strong and thrive, it requires consistent care, reinforcement, and adaptation to changing conditions. Similarly, the success of any transformation effort depends not just on its execution but on its ability to endure and flourish over time.

In the Catalyst Framework, the Sustain phase ensures that the transformation mindset becomes embedded in an organization's behaviors, systems, and culture. Without this phase, even the most successful initiatives risk losing momentum, reverting to old patterns, or fragmenting into isolated successes. Sustainability turns transformation into a way of being, not just a temporary project.

Why Sustainability Matters: Just as neuroplasticity forms lasting neural pathways through repetition, organizations must continuously reinforce the behaviors that drive transformation to ensure that they become the new default.

What This Chapter Covers

This chapter delves into the strategies and tools needed to ensure the transformation mindset sticks. By connecting neuroplasticity principles to organizational systems, you will learn how to:

1. Reinforce the transformation mindset and embed it into daily practices.

2. Scale success across teams, departments, and the entire organization.

3. Use feedback and monitoring tools to track long-term success and make necessary adjustments.

4. Foster leadership alignment to ensure that transformation is championed across all levels of the organization.

By the end of this chapter, you'll have a clear roadmap for sustaining transformation and ensuring the Catalyst Framework continues to deliver lasting value.

Techniques for Ensuring the Transformation Mindset Endures

Sustaining the transformation mindset requires intentional strategies that reinforce new behaviors, foster adaptability, and align efforts with long-term goals. The key to reinforcement is consistency. Just as new neural pathways require repetition to become ingrained, organizational behaviors must be consistently nurtured to prevent regression.

1. Reinforce the Rewired Mindset

Embedding a new mindset doesn't end with execution—it requires continuous reinforcement, especially as organizational focus shifts, leadership changes, or external pressures arise. In the Sustain phase of the Catalyst Framework, the goal is not just to reinforce behaviors, but to ensure that reinforcement mechanisms themselves evolve to remain relevant, resonant, and effective.

Reinforcement at this stage must become more strategic, moving beyond early-stage rituals and recognitions into a **systemic rhythm of cultural renewal**. The behaviors that were once novel must now feel second nature, but that naturalization only happens through deliberate design.

How Reinforcement Evolves in Sustain Phase

From Events to Embedded Routines:

Early-stage celebrations and spotlight moments are powerful for momentum. But in the Sustain phase, reinforcement must shift from being event-driven to **process-integrated**—woven into performance reviews, onboarding, and team check-ins.

From Surface-Level to Deep Alignment:

Recognition should go beyond generic praise to **deeply align with organizational values and strategic objectives**. Reinforce not just what was done, but why it mattered.

From One-Time Narratives to Ongoing Storytelling:

Stories shared during execution become the **foundation for cultural memory**. In the Sustain phase, leaders should continue telling, updating, and evolving these stories so that new employees and teams connect with the transformation journey.

From Individual to Systemic Feedback:

While individual shout-outs are still valuable, system-level reinforcement— through dashboards, performance metrics, and team-based reviews— ensures lasting visibility and accountability.

Example:

A healthcare company that had successfully implemented team-based care initially celebrated early adopters with recognition awards. In the sustain phase, they integrated team-based care behaviors into manager scorecards, employee training, and annual reviews—ensuring the behavior wasn't just encouraged but expected and supported at scale.

2. Sustaining Rituals Without Losing Relevance

Periodically Refresh Rituals:

Review existing rituals (daily huddles, recognition moments, review meetings) and ask: Are they still serving their purpose? Update formats, rotate facilitators, or refocus the agenda to prevent ritual fatigue.

Tie Rituals to What Matters Now:

As business goals shift, so must the focus of rituals. A daily huddle originally centered on cross-functional collaboration might evolve to focus on customer impact or sustainability outcomes.

Empower Teams to Own Their Rituals:

Give teams autonomy to adapt rituals to their context. When teams co-create or evolve their own routines, they take greater ownership of sustaining change.

Recognize the Ritual Itself:

In long-term transformation, it's valuable to occasionally step back and celebrate the consistency of the ritual itself—calling attention to the discipline and commitment it represents.

Example:

A global tech company initially introduced weekly "Innovation Hours" during execution, where teams pitched ideas and explored improvements. By the second year, participation had dropped. To sustain impact, leaders worked with teams to rebrand the hour as "Customer Fix Friday", linking the ritual directly to client-facing improvements. Engagement surged again, and the ritual continued as a valued part of the culture.

3. Maintain Leadership Alignment

Leaders are the cornerstone of sustaining transformation. If leadership isn't aligned, efforts risk fragmentation and a loss of direction. Consistent leadership behavior reinforces change at every level of the organization.

Example: Leadership Alignment in a Financial Institution

A financial institution transitioning to digital-first services conducted quarterly alignment workshops for senior leaders. These sessions focused on aligning leadership behaviors with the organization's transformation goals, ensuring consistent messaging and actions across departments.

Practical Steps for Leadership Alignment:

1. **Regular Check-Ins**: Schedule leadership meetings to align on transformation priorities and challenges.

2. **Model the Mindset**: Leaders should demonstrate desired behaviors, such as collaboration or adaptability, at every opportunity.

3. **Communicate Transparently**: Use town halls, newsletters, or one-on-one conversations to share progress and maintain alignment.

Pro Tip: Empower leaders to act as transformation ambassadors, reinforcing the mindset across their teams.

4. Monitor and Adjust for Long-Term Relevance

Sustaining transformation doesn't mean freezing the organization in a post-change state—it means building the **capacity to adapt continuously** while staying true to the transformation's core principles.

In the Sustain phase, monitoring shifts from short-term execution tracking to **long-term cultural health checks and strategic recalibration.** The goal is to ensure the organization doesn't drift back to old patterns or stagnate under outdated routines.

What Monitoring Looks Like in the Sustain Phase

- **Evaluate Cultural Vital Signs**

    Go beyond operational metrics and ask: *Are people still aligned with the transformation mindset? Are the desired behaviors still alive in the culture?* Use culture audits, employee listening, and leadership reviews to assess cultural drift or fatigue.

- **Recalibrate for Relevance**

    Periodically revisit earlier decisions—what worked during execution may no longer fit new priorities. Sustain-phase organizations have the maturity to retire, revise, or refresh practices without undermining transformation.

- **Listen for Signals of Regression**

    Watch for early warning signs that momentum is fading—rituals becoming mechanical, KPIs being gamed, or silos re-emerging. Address these patterns proactively.

Example:

A professional services firm, two years into its transformation journey, noticed a dip in cross-functional collaboration. An internal audit revealed that while the language of collaboration remained, the structures supporting it had eroded. Leadership reintroduced team-based goal-setting and updated digital collaboration tools, reinvigorating the behavior without restarting the transformation from scratch.

Sustainability Insight:

The Sustain phase requires organizations to operate like gardeners, not architects—constantly tending to what was planted, pruning what no longer serves, and adapting to changing seasons.

Reflection for Readers

- Which of these techniques resonates most with your organization's current challenges?

- How might rituals, recognition programs, or leadership alignment strengthen your efforts to sustain transformation?

Scaling Success: Applying the Catalyst Framework Organization-Wide

Transformation is not a singular event but a continuous process. To make transformation stick, it must scale beyond isolated teams and departments. Achieving organizational-wide success requires intentional efforts to align the mindset, behaviors, and practices across all levels of the organization.

The key to scaling transformation lies in creating systems, processes, and touchpoints that facilitate the spread of the transformation mindset. It's about ensuring that everyone, from senior leadership to frontline employees, is aligned with the vision and the behaviors that will sustain change. The execution is just the first step; scaling ensures that the new mindset becomes ingrained in the organization's DNA, fostering a culture of continuous improvement.

1. Identifying Early Adopters and Champions

As transformation takes root, early adopters and champions play a critical role in spreading the new mindset. These individuals or teams are typically more open to change and can serve as role models for others. Their influence is invaluable in scaling transformation efforts, as they inspire confidence and motivate others to follow suit.

Example: Scaling Agile Practices in a Global Consulting Firm

In a global consulting firm transitioning to agile methodologies, leadership identified a group of early adopters in the organization who were naturally inclined to embrace new ways of working. These agile champions were tasked with mentoring others and providing support as agile practices were introduced across various departments. They hosted workshops, created learning materials, and shared their experiences to make the transition smoother for other teams.

Key Actions:

1. **Identify Influencers:** Look for individuals who naturally gravitate toward transformation and are passionate about driving change.

2. **Equip Champions:** Provide champions with the tools, training, and support needed to mentor others.

3. **Recognize Early Wins:** Celebrate success stories from these champions to inspire others to adopt similar practices.

2. Standardizing Practices While Maintaining Flexibility

While consistency is important in scaling transformation, organizations must ensure they allow room for flexibility. Over-standardization can hinder innovation, so it's critical to strike a balance between maintaining core principles and allowing teams to adapt practices to their local contexts. This approach fosters alignment while enabling agility.

Example: Customer-Centric Transformation in a Telecom Company

A telecom company worked to scale its customer-centricity transformation. While customer service protocols and goals were standardized across the company, employees were empowered to personalize their interactions with clients based on local customer needs. This approach led to stronger customer relationships, improved satisfaction, and better retention rates.

Key Actions:

1. **Identify Core Principles:** Determine the core practices or behaviors that must be standardized across the organization to ensure alignment.

2. **Allow Customization:** Empower teams to adapt standardized practices to their local contexts, making sure they resonate with regional needs.

3. **Monitor Outcomes:** Use data and feedback to ensure that adaptations are effective while still aligning with broader organizational goals.

3. Leveraging Technology for Seamless Scaling

Technology can be a powerful enabler for scaling transformation, providing the infrastructure needed to track progress, communicate effectively, and maintain alignment across the organization. Digital platforms allow leaders to monitor real-time data, share best practices, and streamline processes, making scaling more manageable and transparent.

Example: Scaling Digital Transformation in a Global Retail Chain

A global retail chain used a centralized platform to track the progress of its digital transformation across regions. The platform allowed leadership to monitor key metrics, communicate directly with teams, and share success stories. By leveraging technology, the company was able to scale its digital initiatives efficiently while ensuring consistency in execution.

Key Actions:

1. **Implement Centralized Tools:** Use project management, communication, and analytics tools to facilitate transparency and collaboration.

2. **Share Success Stories Digitally:** Create platforms for teams to share their successes, challenges, and insights with others.

3. **Track Metrics in Real Time:** Use dashboards and metrics to monitor progress and ensure alignment across all regions or departments.

4. Building Momentum Through Early Wins

Early wins are crucial for sustaining momentum during transformation. They serve as proof of concept, demonstrating that the changes being implemented are having a positive impact. Recognizing and celebrating these early successes creates enthusiasm, boosts morale, and builds confidence in the transformation process. Early wins provide tangible evidence that the transformation mindset is working, motivating teams to keep pushing forward.

Example: Scaling Digital Adoption in a Global Bank

A global bank focused on transitioning to digital-first services celebrated every milestone, no matter how small, to keep teams motivated. For example, the successful launch of a new mobile banking feature was celebrated as a major win, with leadership publicly recognizing the team behind it. This recognition reinforced the belief that digital transformation was worth the effort and sparked further innovation across the organization.

Key Actions:

1. **Set Short-Term Goals:** Establish achievable, measurable milestones that show progress and give teams something to strive for.

2. **Celebrate Wins:** Publicly recognize teams or individuals who contribute to these early successes, making them visible to the whole organization.

3. **Use Wins as Leverage:** Use success stories to build enthusiasm and encourage other teams to adopt transformation practices.

5. Empowering Teams to Lead Change

Empowering teams to take ownership of transformation efforts is key to scaling. When individuals are given autonomy and responsibility, they are more likely to invest in the success of the transformation. Teams should not just follow directives but actively shape how the transformation unfolds. By fostering a sense of ownership, organizations tap into the creativity, innovation, and commitment of their employees.

Example: Empowering Employees in a Tech Firm's Agile Transformation

A tech firm undergoing an agile transformation empowered cross-functional teams to experiment with different agile practices. Teams had the freedom to decide which methods would work best for them and could adapt processes to their specific needs. This autonomy led to more rapid adoption of agile practices across the organization, as teams felt a greater sense of ownership in the process.

Key Actions:

1. **Delegate Decision-Making:** Allow teams to take ownership of key transformation decisions, giving them the flexibility to adapt to local needs.

2. **Provide Support, Not Micromanagement:** Ensure that teams have the resources, training, and support they need without being over-controlled.

3. **Celebrate Team Innovation:** Recognize teams for innovative ideas and solutions that contribute to the broader transformation.

6. Scaling Leadership Alignment Across the Organization

Leadership alignment is critical for sustaining transformation at scale. If leaders at all levels are not fully committed to the transformation or fail to model the desired behaviors, the transformation will lose momentum. It's essential for leaders to be on the same page, communicate consistently, and actively demonstrate their commitment to the transformation mindset.

Example: Leadership Alignment in a Multinational Retailer

A multinational retailer undergoing a customer-centric transformation conducted regular alignment workshops for senior leaders. These workshops focused on ensuring that leadership at all levels was on board with the transformation goals and behaviors. Leaders participated in these sessions to align on key messages, share progress, and demonstrate their commitment to customer-centricity. This ensured that the transformation remained a priority and that all leaders were actively reinforcing the same messages.

Key Actions:

1. **Conduct Leadership Workshops:** Hold regular sessions to align leadership on the transformation goals and ensure they are communicating the same vision.

2. **Model Desired Behaviors:** Leaders must actively demonstrate the behaviors they expect from their teams, setting the example for others to follow.

3. **Foster Transparent Communication:** Ensure that leaders communicate progress, challenges, and successes transparently to build trust and credibility.

Reflection for Readers:

- How can you leverage early adopters to scale the transformation mindset in your organization?

- What tools or strategies could help you balance consistency with adaptability across teams or departments?

Tying Neuroplasticity to Sustainability

The science of neuroplasticity has been a recurring thread throughout this book—showing how repeated behaviors, reinforcement, and exposure create lasting change in the brain. In the Sustain phase, these same principles guide how organizations embed and preserve transformation over time.

At this stage, it's no longer about introducing new pathways—it's about **maintaining and strengthening them**.

What Sustained Neuroplasticity Looks Like Organizationally:

- **Reinforcement becomes rhythm.** Recognition and repetition are no longer one-time events; they are institutionalized into performance systems, leadership behaviors, and cultural norms.

- **Exposure becomes embedded**. Cross-functional collaboration, external learning, and diverse thinking are built into how teams operate—not just as initiatives, but as expected ways of working.

- **Habits become culture**. What began as deliberate behavior becomes identity—how people describe "how we do things here."

Example:

A retail company that had adopted customer-first practices continued to evolve these behaviors over five years—not by introducing new initiatives, but by reinforcing, celebrating, and adapting what already worked. The result wasn't just sustained change—it was a new cultural default.

In essence, sustaining transformation is organizational neuroplasticity in action. The wiring has changed. Now, it must be maintained.

Reflection for Readers

- How can you use repetition, reinforcement, and exposure to sustain your transformation goals?

- What steps can you take today to ensure the new behaviors you've introduced are becoming part of your organization's culture?

Tools for Tracking Long-Term Success

As transformation moves into the Sustain phase, organizations need tools that go beyond operational execution. These tools must provide ongoing visibility into cultural health, behavioral consistency, and strategic alignment.

The purpose is not just to measure activity, but to assess whether the spirit of the transformation is still alive—and where attention is needed to keep it that way.

Essential Tools for Sustainability Monitoring

- **Cultural Pulse Surveys**

  Lightweight, frequent surveys that check for alignment with values, mindsets, and desired behaviors. They surface early signs of disengagement, resistance, or cultural drift.

- **Transformation Scorecards**

  Dashboards that track long-term metrics—not just performance, but behavioral indicators (e.g., cross-team collaboration rates, participation in innovation programs, customer-centric actions).

- **Ritual Health Checklists**

  Regular reviews of key rituals and routines to evaluate whether they are still meaningful, energizing, and aligned with strategy—or have become stale or mechanical.

- **Narrative Audits**

  Assess whether the dominant stories being told in the organization still reflect the transformation mindset. Are leaders reinforcing the right beliefs? Are old anti-stories resurfacing?

- **Sustainability Retrospectives**

  Annual or biannual cross-functional reviews focused not on past performance but on the health of the transformation effort itself—what's enduring, what's fading, and what needs to evolve.

Example:

A global CPG company created a "Transformation Heat Map" updated quarterly by business unit leaders. It tracked behavioral metrics like idea-sharing, experimentation frequency, and learning engagement—alongside operational KPIs. The map highlighted where transformation was thriving and where renewed focus was needed.

Sustainability Insight:

If transformation is to endure, it must be monitored like a living system. Tools should be lightweight but insightful—designed not to control, but to inform and adapt.

Reflection for Readers

- What long-term signals—not just KPIs—could help you assess the health of your transformation?

- Which tools could help you track both cultural alignment and behavioral consistency over time?

- How might you build lightweight rituals (e.g., dashboards, retrospectives, narrative audits) into your transformation to ensure it stays alive, relevant, and adaptive?

Real-Life Example: Sustaining Transformation in a Retail Chain

Challenge:

A retail chain set out to transition to a digital-first strategy to stay competitive in a rapidly evolving marketplace. The initial rollout of e-commerce initiatives delivered promising results, but sustaining the transformation proved more difficult.

Over time, employees began to revert to legacy practices, such as prioritizing in-store promotions over online engagement. These habits undermined the emerging digital culture, revealing that without a long-term reinforcement plan, early success would stall.

Catalyst Framework Application: Sustain Phase in Action

To preserve momentum and embed the change into daily operations, the company activated the Sustain phase of the Catalyst Framework. Their focus shifted from rolling out new initiatives to institutionalizing behaviors, building peer-driven support systems, and maintaining long-term visibility

1. Reinforcing the Mindset

Leaders knew that sustaining transformation required ongoing emotional connection and narrative reinforcement. They highlighted real-world examples to keep the digital-first mindset alive:

- Customer Stories: Testimonials from customers who experienced seamless online shopping were shared across the company, helping employees see the human impact of their efforts.

- Employee Highlights: Newsletters and town halls celebrated team members who excelled in digital adoption, showcasing how individual actions contributed to the larger strategy.

2. Scaling Success Through Peer Mentorship

Rather than relying solely on top-down communication, the company created a mentorship model to scale and sustain adoption:

- Early adopters were trained as mentors and partnered with underperforming locations.

- Mentors received tools, leadership coaching, and resources to help other teams integrate digital practices into their daily workflows.

- Peer-learning sessions were hosted regularly, creating a culture of horizontal knowledge transfer and shared accountability.

3. Monitoring Progress Through Visibility and Transperancy

To prevent drift, the organization invested in clear, ongoing measurement of transformation behaviors:

- Live dashboards displayed metrics like online sales growth, digital customer satisfaction, and employee engagement with e-commerce tools.

- Teams across all regions could access and track progress, sparking friendly competition and cross-location learning.

Outcome: Transformation Sustained

Within two years, the retailer successfully embedded its digital-first culture, achieving lasting impact:

- 40% Increase in Online Sales, driven by consistent behavior reinforcement and wide adoption of digital tools.

- Enhanced Customer Experience, with customers praising seamless integration across online and in-store channels.

- Stronger Employee Engagement, with 85% of employees reporting confidence in the company's digital direction.

Key Takeaways from the Case Study:

1. Reinforcement must evolve: Storytelling and recognition aren't one-time acts—they must become part of how the organization thinks, shares, and celebrates.

2. Peer-driven scaling works: Empowering early adopters to lead others creates sustainable, grassroots momentum.

3. Visibility fuels discipline: Transparent tracking ensures that transformation doesn't drift—everyone can see progress, gaps, and where to course-correct.

Reflection for Readers

- What lessons from this example could you apply to sustain transformation efforts in your organization?

- How might mentorship programs, storytelling, or transparent dashboards strengthen long-term adoption of new behaviors?

Making Transformation Enduring

Transformation isn't a one-time leap—it's a continuous commitment. While strategy, design, and execution launch the journey, it's the ability to **sustain change over time** that determines whether transformation becomes embedded or fades away.

In the Sustain phase of the Catalyst Framework, the focus shifts from **driving momentum** to **maintaining maturity**. Habits become norms. Rituals become rhythms. And beliefs become culture.

The most successful organizations aren't the ones that transform once—they're the ones that make transformation a **way of being**. They don't chase change reactively; they build the capacity to **adapt proactively**, renewing their mindset and methods as the world evolves.

Key Lessons for Enduring Transformation

- **Consistency outlasts intensity**. Sustained change comes from small actions repeated over time—not big campaigns that burn out quickly.

- **Culture carries the transformation forward**. When behaviors are reinforced through storytelling, rituals, systems, and leadership modeling, change no longer needs constant top-down management—it becomes self-sustaining.

- **Renewal is part of the process**. What worked last year might not serve tomorrow. Resilient organizations revisit, refine, and reimagine—without losing sight of their core purpose.

Transformation endures not because it is perfect, but because it is **persistent, visible, and lived daily.**

As you move forward, ask not just how to change—but how to keep the right changes alive.

Looking Ahead: Leading Beyond the Organization

As we conclude the Sustain phase, it's important to recognize that transformation doesn't stop at the walls of your organization. The Catalyst Framework—and the mindset it fosters—can shape not just teams and businesses, but entire industries, communities, and systems.

In the final chapter, we'll explore how leaders can extend their impact beyond their organizations—championing the transformation mindset as a broader movement. This is where transformation becomes not just a strategy—but a legacy.

Reflection for Readers

- What will it take for your transformation to endure—beyond leadership changes, strategic shifts, or external pressure?

- Which rituals, behaviors, or systems in your organization are ready to be reinforced, refreshed, or retired?

- How can you embed transformation into culture—so it's not something you manage, but something you live?

- What stories will your teams tell one year from now about how the change held on—and why?

Chapter Summary

- The Sustain phase of the Catalyst Framework ensures that transformation becomes embedded, not temporary—turning new behaviors into lasting cultural norms.

- Sustainability is about consistency, adaptability, and reinforcement. Just as neuroplasticity wires new brain patterns through repetition, organizations must reinforce transformation until it becomes second nature.

- Four key strategies to sustain transformation:

  1. Reinforce the mindset: Move beyond initial recognition toward embedded rituals, aligned scorecards, and strategic storytelling that connect everyday behavior to transformation goals.

  2. Keep rituals relevant: Regularly refresh and localize rituals to maintain engagement and reflect evolving priorities.

  3. Maintain leadership alignment: Leaders must model, communicate, and champion the transformation continuously across all levels.

  4. Monitor & adapt: Use cultural audits, dashboards, and narrative reviews to detect drift and recalibrate without losing momentum.

- Scaling transformation requires:

  1. Empowering early adopters and champions

  2. Balancing standardization with local flexibility

  3. Leveraging technology for visibility, communication, and feedback

  4. Using early wins and recognition to build belief and momentum

- Case studies show that when reinforcement becomes systemic, storytelling remains alive, and rituals evolve with context, transformation sticks—and spreads.

- Sustaining transformation is organizational neuroplasticity in action: reinforcing new pathways until they become identity.

Sustainability isn't about preserving a fixed state—it's about building a culture that can continuously evolve without losing its core.

Action Exercises: Applying the Insights

These exercises are designed to help leaders and teams sustain the momentum of transformation by embedding behaviors, reinforcing rituals, and creating visibility around progress. They focus on long-term ownership, cultural reinforcement, and strategic renewal—hallmarks of the Sustain phase of the Catalyst Framework.

1. Create a Sustainability Plan

- Develop a plan to reinforce behaviors, embed practices, and track progress for one of your organization's transformation initiatives.

Steps:

1. Identify a key behavior or practice that aligns with your transformation goals.

   - Example: Regular team collaboration on cross-functional projects.

2. Define how this behavior will be reinforced through rituals, recognition, or tools.

   - Example: Weekly team huddles and public recognition for successful collaboration efforts.

3. Establish a timeline for monitoring progress and evaluating impact.

   - Example: Quarterly reviews to assess collaboration outcomes and identify improvements.

Outcome: A clear roadmap for sustaining new behaviors over the long term.

2. Conduct a Reflection Session

Objective: Facilitate a team-based reflection to assess progress, celebrate wins, and identify opportunities for continued transformation.

Steps:

1. Schedule a session with your team and provide the following prompts in advance:

   - What progress have we made toward our transformation goals?

   - What challenges have we encountered, and how can we address them?

   - What successes can we celebrate, and how can we build on them?

2. Facilitate an open discussion, ensuring all voices are heard.

3. Document key insights and agree on next steps to maintain momentum.

Outcome: A shared understanding of transformation progress and a renewed sense of collective ownership.

3. Design a Sustainability Dashboard

Objective: Create a dashboard to track progress on transformation goals, helping teams stay aligned and accountable.

Steps:

1. Identify key metrics aligned with your transformation goals (e.g., employee engagement, customer satisfaction, innovation activity).

2. Use tools like Excel, Tableau, or Google Sheets to design a visual, up-to-date dashboard.

3. Include a mix of leading indicators (e.g., training participation) and lagging indicators (e.g., business outcomes).

4. Share the dashboard during team check-ins or retrospectives to maintain visibility and alignment.

Outcome: A dynamic tool that supports ongoing monitoring and adaptive decision-making.

4. Run a Transformation Audit

Objective: Evaluate whether transformation efforts are being sustained across your organization and identify areas for renewal.

Steps:

1. Develop an audit framework including key focus areas (e.g., behaviors, systems, leadership, culture).

2. Gather insights via surveys, interviews, or focus groups with diverse stakeholders.

3. Analyze findings to surface what's working, what's fading, and where drift may be occurring.

4. Present results to leadership and create an action plan to address gaps and reinforce what matters.

Outcome: A clear picture of transformation health—and a practical guide for sustaining progress.

5. Scale Success Through Peer Learning

Objective: Encourage peer-led learning to scale transformation mindsets and practices across teams.

Steps:

1. Identify teams or individuals who have exemplified the transformation mindset in action.

2. Organize peer-learning sessions where these teams share lessons and successful practices.

3. Facilitate group discussion to adapt ideas for different business contexts.

4. Capture insights in a shared repository or playbook to inspire ongoing collaboration.

Outcome: A grassroots mechanism for reinforcing behaviors and scaling transformation across the organization.

Reflection for Readers

- Which of these sustainability exercises feels most relevant to your transformation journey right now?

- How might creating a **sustainability plan**, conducting a **transformation audit**, or launching a **peer-learning series** help you ensure long-term impact?

Chapter 12:

From Mindset to Movement:
The Conclusion

Transformation begins with the individual—the rewiring of beliefs, the adoption of new behaviors, and aligning actions with purpose. However, its true potential lies in its ability to ripple outward—through teams, organizations, industries, and society. When transformation moves from a personal mindset to a collective movement, it becomes a powerful force for progress.

Imagine tossing a pebble into a still pond. The ripples start small but grow wider, touching everything in their path. Each ripple represents an individual's transformation journey, creating momentum that inspires others to think differently, act boldly, and lead change. Movements begin with small, intentional shifts that gain traction and scale over time.

This chapter explores how leaders can scale the transformation mindset, creating systemic change beyond their organization. You'll learn how to champion cultural shifts, envision a future where transformation is second nature, and extend the impact of the Catalyst Framework beyond your organization. By the end, you'll feel empowered to lead not just within your team, but as a change-maker in your community and industry.

What This Chapter Covers:

- **Leadership as a Catalyst**: How leaders can inspire and embody the transformation mindset.

- **Scaling Cultural Shifts**: Strategies for embedding transformation principles across organizations.

- **Envisioning the Future**: A vision for workplaces where adaptability, collaboration, and purpose drive success.

- **Impact Beyond the Workplace**: How the transformation mindset influences industries and societal challenges.

- **Your Role in the Movement**: Practical steps to lead your own transformation movement.

Leaders as Champions of the Transformation Mindset

Leadership is the linchpin of transformation. Leaders set the tone, model behaviors, and inspire action. To champion the transformation mindset, leaders must move beyond directive leadership and become catalysts for growth, empowering those around them to think, act, and lead differently.

1. Modeling the Transformation Mindset

Leadership is most effective when it's lived, not just communicated. Leaders who embody the traits of the transformation mindset—adaptability, curiosity, resilience, and empowerment—serve as role models, inspiring others to follow.

Example: The CEO of a multinational telecom company led a digital overhaul. She actively participated in workshops, experimented with agile methodologies, and openly shared her learning journey. This visible commitment inspired her leadership team, creating a ripple effect through the organization. Within two years, the company achieved a 30% increase in customer satisfaction and faster time-to-market for digital services.

Practical Tip:

- Reflect on your leadership behaviors. Are you modeling the transformation mindset? Identify one behavior to model consistently, such as seeking feedback or championing innovation.

2. Inspiring Action Through Vision

A compelling vision is the North Star for transformation. Leaders who articulate a clear and inspiring vision help their teams connect with the "why" behind transformation and understand their role in it.

Example: A logistics firm transformed its culture with the vision of "Delivering excellence to every doorstep." This unifying statement inspired employees across teams to prioritize customer satisfaction. Leaders reinforced the vision through storytelling, sharing customer testimonials that demonstrated the impact of their work.

Practical Tip:

- Craft a transformation vision that is both aspirational and actionable. Share it consistently through team meetings, storytelling, and visual communications (e.g., posters, newsletters).

3. Empowering Others to Lead

Transformation becomes sustainable when leaders empower their teams to take ownership. Empowerment creates a multiplier effect, enabling individuals at every level to act as agents of transformation.

Case Study: A retail chain empowered store managers to localize digital marketing campaigns. This decentralized approach allowed managers to adapt to local customer preferences while aligning with the broader organizational vision. The result was a 25% increase in online sales.

Practical Tip:

- Delegate meaningful responsibilities to team members and provide the resources they need to succeed. Celebrate small wins and encourage experimentation to reinforce innovation and ownership.

4. Building Emotional Connections

Leaders who connect emotionally with their teams foster trust and inspire commitment to transformation. By sharing personal stories, expressing vulnerability, and demonstrating empathy, leaders build relationships that drive engagement and alignment.

Example: During a major restructuring, the CEO of a financial services firm shared her own challenges adapting to change. Her transparency created a safe space for employees to voice concerns and engage in the transformation process.

Practical Tip:

- Share personal stories that illustrate your commitment to the transformation mindset. Actively listen to your team's concerns and work collaboratively to address them.

From Individual Mindsets to Cultural Shifts

Cultural transformation begins with individual changes but requires systemic alignment to scale. While an individual's transformation can spark a ripple effect, it is the alignment of systems, processes, and behaviors that turns those ripples into a powerful wave of organizational change.

1. The Ripple Effect of Individual Transformation

When individuals embrace the transformation mindset, their behaviors influence those around them, creating a ripple effect. Over time, these ripples converge to shift the organization's culture.

Example: At a biotech company, a single team fostered curiosity by hosting "What if?" sessions. The success of their innovations inspired other departments to adopt similar practices, turning curiosity into a company-wide norm and increasing R&D efficiency by 20%.

Practical Tip:

- Encourage teams to share successes and lessons learned. Create platforms for collaboration and knowledge sharing, such as innovation forums or company-wide knowledge-sharing sessions.

2. Designing for Cultural Transformation

Cultural shifts don't happen by chance—they must be intentionally designed. Leaders must embed the transformation mindset into systems, processes, and rituals to ensure lasting impact.

Key Strategies for Cultural Transformation:

- **Rituals**: Introduce practices that reinforce desired behaviors.

  - *Example*: A manufacturing firm transitioning to lean operations instituted daily stand-up meetings where teams reviewed wins, challenges, and opportunities.

- **Incentives**: Align performance metrics and rewards with transformation goals.

  - *Example*: A financial institution redesigned its performance appraisal system to prioritize collaboration and adaptability.

- **Training and Development**: Offer continuous learning opportunities to build skills supporting the transformation mindset.

  - *Example*: A retail chain provided workshops on digital literacy to empower employees during its shift to omnichannel operations.

Practical Tip:

- Audit your organization's systems and practices to identify misalignments with the transformation mindset and adjust them accordingly.

3. Overcoming Resistance to Cultural Change

Cultural shifts often face resistance, especially from individuals threatened by new ways of working. Addressing these concerns with empathy and transparency is crucial to maintaining momentum.

Example: During a shift to hybrid work, a manufacturing company faced resistance from managers used to in-person oversight. Leadership held open forums, provided training on managing remote teams, and highlighted the benefits of flexibility. Over time, these efforts helped shift the culture to embrace hybrid work models.

Practical Strategies:

- Identify sources of resistance early and engage with teams to understand their concerns.

- Involve employees in designing solutions to address their challenges.
- Communicate transparently about the "why" behind the transformation and provide regular updates.

Pro Tip:

- Pair resistant individuals with transformation champions to foster peer-driven support.

4. Measuring Cultural Transformation

Tracking cultural transformation ensures alignment with organizational goals and progress over time. Metrics like employee engagement, collaboration rates, and customer satisfaction can indicate how the culture is evolving.

Example: A healthcare organization transitioning to team-based care tracked collaboration rates through shared metrics such as patient outcomes and project completion. Regular reflection sessions provided qualitative insights into cultural shifts.

Practical Tip:

- Use a combination of quantitative (e.g., survey results, project milestones) and qualitative (e.g., focus groups) feedback to assess cultural transformation.

Vision for the Future: A Transformation-Ready Workplace

Imagine a workplace where transformation is not a project, but a way of life. In this future, organizations are dynamic, adaptable, and purpose-driven, characterized by a culture that embraces change as an opportunity, not a threat. Transformation becomes second nature, woven into daily operations, decision-making, and collaboration.

Key Characteristics of Transformation-Ready Workplaces:

1. Adaptability: Teams pivot seamlessly, leveraging disruption for innovation.

2. Collaboration: Cross-functional teams work together to achieve shared goals.

3. Continuous Learning: Employees are empowered to grow, experiment, and innovate.

4. Purpose-Driven Action: Work is aligned with values that inspire meaningful impact.

The Broader Impact of Transformation-Ready Workplaces

Organizations that embed transformation into their culture don't just thrive—they drive progress beyond their walls. By aligning business goals with societal impact, these organizations address challenges like sustainability, inclusion, and equity.

Example: A logistics firm adopted a transformation-first culture and achieved carbon-neutral operations. Partners in its supply chain followed suit, leading to a 25% reduction in emissions across the network.

Practical Tip:

- Reflect on how your organization's transformation can address broader societal needs while driving business growth.

Transformation doesn't stop at the edge of your org chart. Its power lies in its ability to scale—to influence ecosystems, industries, and entire communities.

Tying Transformation to Broader Change

The transformation mindset extends beyond individual organizations, creating ripple effects that influence industries, communities, and society. When leaders embrace this mindset, they contribute to addressing global challenges and drive progress on a larger scale.

Transforming Industries: Example: A global apparel brand adopted sustainable practices, influencing competitors to follow suit and raising industry standards for eco-friendly practices.

Practical Tip:

- Identify areas where your organization can lead industry-wide change by partnering with competitors or regulators to amplify your impact.

Empowering Communities: **Example**: A telecom company expanded digital access in underserved regions, improving customer experiences while driving business growth.

Practical Tip:

- Reflect on your organization's broader purpose and align your transformation efforts with community needs.

Final Call to Action: Lead Your Movement

You are no longer just a participant in transformation—you are a catalyst.

The mindset you've built, the tools you've practiced, and the systems you've shaped are only the beginning. The real impact begins when you model transformation for others, when your organization becomes a beacon of what's possible, and when your leadership inspires not only results, but replication.

This is your call to lead beyond the boundaries of your job title, your company, or your industry.

To speak the language of possibility in rooms still trapped by fear.

To ask better questions in systems stuck in outdated answers.

To plant seeds of change where none were expected to grow.

The transformation mindset doesn't end here. It begins again—with you.

Reflection for Readers:

- What will it look like for you to lead transformation not just within your team, but across your ecosystem?

- Where can you amplify the mindset—not by launching another project, but by how you show up, listen, and lead?

- What's one behavior, belief, or story you will carry forward—and help others carry too?

- Who around you might be ready to become the next catalyst?

Conclusion: The Catalyst for Change

Sustainable transformation is not built on tools alone. It's built on belief. On repetition. On leadership that dares to be human and systems that dare to evolve.

The Catalyst Framework is more than a model—it's a mirror. A way of seeing yourself and your organization as instruments of change. Not through force. But through consistency, curiosity, and courage.

You don't need a title to start. You only need a moment.

A conversation. A mindset.

And the commitment to keep showing up, long after the spotlight fades.

Transformation is not the work of one hero.

It's the work of many catalysts—quietly, boldly, and relentlessly moving the world forward.

You are now one of them.

Final Reflection: Becoming a Catalyst

Transformation doesn't end here—it begins with your next choice.

Before you turn the final page, pause and reflect:

- What belief will you rewire in yourself first—before asking others to change?

- What daily behavior can you adopt that reflects the transformation mindset—adaptability, curiosity, resilience, or empowerment?

- What ritual will you introduce—or reinforce—in your team to keep change alive?

- Whose mindset might you quietly influence, simply by how you show up?

- What story will you tell—six months from now—about the movement you helped spark?

Write it down. Share it. Live it.

Continuing Your Transformation Journey

Transformation is a continuous practice of learning, reflection, and growth. To deepen your understanding of the science and strategy behind lasting change, here are a few influential resources that complement the ideas explored in this book.

On How Our Brains Adapt and Grow

- *The Brain That Changes Itself* by Norman Doidge
- *Your Brain at Work* by David Rock

On Building Habits and Shaping Behavior

- *Tiny Habits* by BJ Fogg
- *Atomic Habits* by James Clear
- *The Power of Habit* by Charles Duhigg

On Leading Change and Shaping Culture

- *Leading Change* by John P. Kotter
- *The Culture Code* by Daniel Coyle
- *The Fearless Organization* by Amy Edmondson

On Mindset and Continuous Learning

- *Mindset* by Carol Dweck
- *Think Again* by Adam Grant

Bringing the Transformation Mindset to Life

The journey of transformation does not end with reading—it begins when mindsets shift, conversations deepen, and action follows.

To support leaders and organizations in translating these ideas into meaningful change, I offer two signature experiences inspired by *The Transformation Mindset*:

Keynote: The Transformation Mindset Advantage

An inspiring, high-impact session that brings the core principles of the book to life. Through real-world stories, neuroscience insights, and practical lessons, this keynote energizes audiences to embrace adaptability, curiosity, resilience, and empowerment in their leadership and organizational journeys.

Ideal for: Leadership summits, company-wide transformation launches, innovation days, and strategic offsites.

Workshop: Applying the Catalyst Framework

A hands-on, interactive workshop that guides teams through the five phases of the Catalyst Framework—Analyze, Reframe, Design, Execute, and Sustain.

Participants learn how to identify transformation blockers, reframe limiting narratives, and build practical strategies to drive sustainable change.

Ideal for: Change agents, transformation teams, business unit leaders, and cross-functional leadership cohorts.

Both experiences are designed to be practical, energizing, and deeply aligned with the spirit of *The Transformation Mindset*—equipping individuals and organizations to rewire, embed, and lead transformation from within.

If you are ready to turn ideas into action and spark a movement of sustainable change, I look forward to partnering with you.

Connect

For speaking engagements, workshops, and collaborations, please reach out:

✉ Email: **manishpharasi@gmail.com**

🔗 LinkedIn: **https://www.linkedin.com/in/manish-pharasi-a8192b3/**

9 798897 778850